The Official Rails-to-Trails Conservancy Guidebook

2nd Edition

Rail-Trails
Mid-Atlantic

The definitive guide to multiuse trails
in Delaware, Maryland, Virginia,
Washington, D.C., and West Virginia

 WILDERNESS PRESS ... *on the trail since 1967*

Rail-Trails: Mid-Atlantic
2nd Edition
Copyright © 2015 by Rails-to-Trails Conservancy

Maps: Lohnes+Wright; Map data: Environmental Systems Research Institute
Cover design: Scott McGrew
Book design: Annie Long

Library of Congress Cataloging-in-Publication Data

Rail-trails mid-Atlantic : the definitive guide to multi-use trails in Delaware, Maryland, Virginia, West Virginia, and Washington, D.C. / by The Rails-to-Trails Conservancy. — 2nd edition.
    pages cm
  Includes bibliographical references and index.
  ISBN 978-0-89997-795-9 — ISBN 0-89997-795-2
  1. Rail-trails—Delaware—Guidebooks. 2. Rail-trails—Maryland—Guidebooks. 3. Rail-trails—Virginia—Guidebooks. 4. Rail-trails—West Virginia—Guidebooks. 5. Rail-trails—Washington (D.C.)—Guidebooks. 6. Outdoor recreation—Delaware—Guidebooks.
7. Outdoor recreation—Maryland—Guidebooks. 8. Outdoor recreation—Virginia—Guidebooks. 9. Outdoor recreation—West Virginia—Guidebooks. 10. Outdoor recreation—Washington (D.C.)—Guidebooks. I. Rails-to-Trails Conservancy, issuing body.
  GV191.42.D32R35 2015
  796.50975—dc23

                          2015009029

ISBN 9780899977959 (pbk.); 9780899977966 (ebook); 9780899979373 (hardcover)

Published by: **Wilderness Press**
                 An imprint of AdventureKEEN
                 2204 First Avenue South, Suite 102
                 Birmingham, AL 35233
                 800-443-7227; fax 205-326-1012
                 info@wildernesspress.com
                 wildernesspress.com

Visit our website for a complete listing of our books and for ordering information.

Distributed by Publishers Group West

Front cover: High Bridge Trail; courtesy of the Virginia Department of Conservation and Recreation; *Back cover*: Green Mountain Trail; © Rails-to-Trails Conservancy

About Rails-to-Trails Conservancy

Headquartered in Washington, D.C., Rails-to-Trails Conservancy (RTC) is a nonprofit organization dedicated to creating a nationwide network of trails from former rail lines and connecting corridors to build healthier places for healthier people.

Railways helped build America. Spanning from coast to coast, these ribbons of steel linked people, communities, and enterprises, spurring commerce and forging a single nation that bridges a continent. But in recent decades, many of these routes have fallen into disuse, severing communal ties that helped bind Americans together.

When RTC opened its doors in 1986, the rail-trail movement was in its infancy. While there were some 250 miles of open rail-trails in the United States, most projects focused on single, linear routes in rural areas, created for recreation and conservation. RTC sought broader protection for the unused corridors, incorporating rural, suburban, and urban routes.

Year after year, RTC's efforts to protect and align public funding with trail building created an environment that allowed trail advocates in communities across the country to initiate trail projects. These ever-growing ranks of trail professionals, volunteers, and RTC supporters have built momentum for the national rail-trails movement. As the number of supporters multiplied, so did the rail-trails.

Americans now enjoy more than 22,000 miles of open rail-trails, and as they flock to the trails to connect with family members and friends, enjoy nature, and get to places in their local neighborhoods and beyond, their economic prosperity, health, and overall well-being continue to flourish.

A signature endeavor of RTC is **TrailLink.com,** America's portal to these rail-trails as well as other multiuse trails. When RTC launched **TrailLink.com** in 2000, our organization was one of the first to compile such detailed trail information on a national scale. Today, the website continues to play a critical role in both encouraging and satisfying the country's growing need for opportunities to ride, walk, skate, or run for recreation or transportation. This free trail-finder database—which includes detailed descriptions, interactive maps, photo galleries, and first-hand ratings and reviews—can be used as a companion resource to the trails in this guidebook.

The national voice for more than 160,000 members and supporters, RTC is committed to ensuring a better future for America made possible by trails and the connections they inspire. Learn more at **railstotrails.org.**

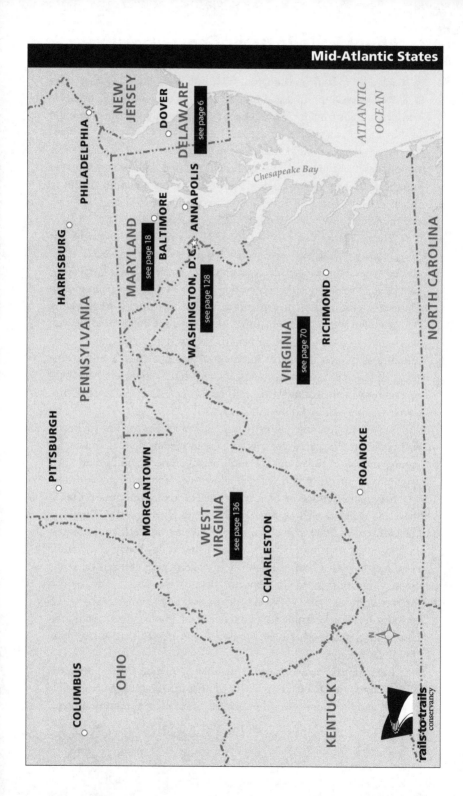

Mid-Atlantic States

ATLANTIC OCEAN

Chesapeake Bay

NEW JERSEY

DELAWARE
DOVER
see page 6

PHILADELPHIA

HARRISBURG

MARYLAND
BALTIMORE
see page 18

ANNAPOLIS
WASHINGTON, D.C.
see page 128

PENNSYLVANIA

PITTSBURGH

MORGANTOWN

VIRGINIA
see page 70

RICHMOND

NORTH CAROLINA

ROANOKE

WEST VIRGINIA
see page 136

CHARLESTON

OHIO

COLUMBUS

KENTUCKY

N

rails-to-trails
conservancy

Table of Contents

DELAWARE 6

MARYLAND 18

Staff Picks

Staff members at Rails-to-Trails Conservancy handpicked the following trails as their favorites, based on such merits as scenic value, unique attractions, bike-friendly communities, and excellent maintenance of the trails and their trailside amenities.

Foreword

For those of you who have already experienced the sheer enjoyment and freedom of riding on a rail-trail, welcome back! You'll find *Rail-Trails: Mid-Atlantic* to be a useful and fun guide to your favorite trails, as well as an introduction to pathways you have yet to travel.

For readers who are discovering for the first time the adventures possible on a rail-trail, thank you for joining the rail-trail movement. Since 1986, Rails-to-Trails Conservancy has been the leading supporter and defender of these priceless public corridors. We are excited to bring you *Rail-Trails: Mid-Atlantic*, so you, too, can enjoy this region's rail-trails, as well as other multiuse trails that provide the same high-quality experience that you expect from a rail-trail.

These hiking and biking trails are ideal ways to connect with your community, with nature, and with your friends and family.

I've found that trails have a way of bringing people together; as you'll see from this book, you have opportunities in every state you visit to get on a great trail. Whether you're looking for a place to exercise, explore, commute, or play, there is a trail in this book for you.

So I invite you to sit back, relax, pick a trail that piques your interest—and then get out, get active, and have some fun. I'll be out on the trails too, so be sure to wave as you go by.

Happy trails,
Keith Laughlin, President
Rails-to-Trails Conservancy

Acknowledgments

Many thanks to the following contributors and to all the trail managers we called on for assistance to ensure the maps, photographs, and trail descriptions are as accurate as possible:

Cindy Dickerson

Eli Griffen

Kathryn Harris

Jennifer Kaleba

Amy Kapp

Timothy Rosner

Laura Stark

Introduction

Of the more than 1,900 rail-trails across the United States, 147 thread through the Mid-Atlantic region of Delaware; Maryland; Virginia; Washington, D.C.; and West Virginia. These routes relate a two-part story: The first speaks to the early years of railroading, while the second showcases efforts by Rails-to-Trails Conservancy, other groups, and their supporters to resurrect these unused railroad corridors as public-use trails. *Rail-Trails: Mid-Atlantic* highlights 57 of the region's diverse trails, each serving as a window into the communities the railroad once served. Some trails delve into the particular history of an area, such as Virginia's Hanging Rock Battlefield Trail, which tells of Civil War battles and the importance of the railroad to the troops. Other trails, such as Maryland's Savage Mill Trail, tell a more docile tale. At its trailhead stands a renovated 1822 textile mill.

In this updated edition, we've also included some of our favorite multiuse trails. These trails were not previously railroad corridors, but many still have the look and feel of the rail-trails that you've come to love. The Mount Vernon Trail in Northern Virginia is a great example of a multiuse trail full of scenic, cultural, and historical charm that is a wonderful corridor to walk, run, skate, or bike.

With the most trails of the region, West Virginia also boasts some of the most rural and unique rail-trails. Not always the flat and even pathways you might expect from rail-trails, West Virginia's trails offer a variety of backwoods treks, such as the Limerock and Green Mountain Trails of the Monongahela National Forest. Complementing these rustic pathways are the well-groomed yet still wild and wonderful Mountain State trails, such as the gorgeous and popular 77-mile Greenbrier River Trail or Deckers Creek Trail in Morgantown, which is part of the Mon River Rail-Trail System.

Next door, Virginia is also a keeper of rail-trail gems. No guide to the area would be complete without featuring the state's southern Virginia Creeper National Recreation Trail, which was inducted into the Rail-Trail Hall of Fame in 2014. In the northern part of the state, right outside the bustle of Washington, D.C., the Washington & Old Dominion Regional Park takes riders out of the city and into rolling farmland and horse country.

Washington, D.C., itself is home to a portion of the Capital Crescent Trail, which begins in suburban Maryland before heading to the historical and trendy Georgetown neighborhood. And in the state best known for its crabs and waterways, Maryland's Cross Island Trail is a coastal sojourn. The only closer you could get would be to meander on Delaware's Junction & Breakwater Trail, which sits in the heart of the state's recreational beach area.

No matter which route in *Rail-Trails: Mid-Atlantic* you decide to try, you'll be touching on the heart of the community that helped build it and the history that first brought the rails to the region.

What Is a Rail-Trail?

Rail-trails are multiuse public paths built along former railroad corridors. Most often flat or following a gentle grade, they are suited to walking, running, cycling, mountain biking, in-line skating, cross-country skiing, horseback riding, and wheelchair use. Since the 1960s, Americans have created more than 22,000 miles of rail-trails throughout the country.

These extremely popular recreation and transportation corridors traverse urban, suburban, and rural landscapes. Many preserve historic landmarks, while others serve as wildlife conservation corridors, linking isolated parks and establishing greenways in developed areas. Rail-trails also stimulate local economies by boosting tourism and promoting trailside businesses.

What Is a Rail-with-Trail?

A rail-with-trail is a public path that parallels a still-active rail line. Some run adjacent to high-speed, scheduled trains, often linking public transportation stations, while others follow tourist routes and slow-moving excursion trains. Many share an easement, separated from the rails by extensive fencing. More than 240 rails-with-trails currently exist in the United States.

How to Use This Book

*R*ail-Trails: *Mid-Atlantic* provides the information you'll need to plan a rewarding trail trek. With words to inspire you and maps to chart your path, it makes choosing the best route a breeze. Following are some of the highlights.

Maps

You'll find three levels of maps in this book: an **overall regional map, state locator maps,** and **detailed trail maps.**

The Mid-Atlantic region includes Delaware; Maryland; Virginia; Washington, D.C.; and West Virginia. Also included in this guide are two trails that run predominantly through Pennsylvania but serve as important and prominent connections to Maryland and West Virginia. Each chapter details a particular state's network of trails, marked on locator maps in the chapter introduction. Use these maps to find the trails nearest to you, or select several neighboring trails and plan a weekend hiking or biking excursion. Once you find a trail on a state locator map, simply flip to the corresponding page number for a full description. Accompanying trail maps mark each route's access roads, trailheads, parking areas, restrooms, and other defining features.

Key to Map Icons

Parking

Drinking water

Restrooms

Trail Descriptions

Trails are listed in alphabetical order within each chapter. Each description leads off with a set of summary information, including trail endpoints and mileage, a roughness index, the trail surface, and possible uses.

The map and summary information list the trail endpoints (either a city, street, or more specific location), with suggested points from which to start and finish. Additional access points are marked on the maps and mentioned in the trail descriptions. The maps and descriptions also highlight available amenities, including parking and restrooms, as well as such area attractions as shops, services, museums, parks, and stadiums. Trail length is listed in miles.

Each trail bears a roughness index rating from 1 to 3. A rating of 1 indicates a smooth, level surface that is accessible to users of all ages and abilities. A 2 rating means the surface may be loose and/or uneven and could pose a problem for road bikes and wheelchairs. A 3 rating suggests a rough surface that is only recommended for mountain bikers and hikers. Surfaces can range from asphalt or concrete to ballast, cinder, crushed stone, gravel, grass, dirt, and/or sand. Where relevant, trail descriptions address alternating surface conditions.

All trails are open to pedestrians, and most allow bicycles, except where noted in the trail summary or description. The summary also indicates wheelchair access. Other possible uses include in-line skating, fishing, horseback riding, mountain biking, and cross-country skiing. While most trails are off-limits to motor vehicles, some local trail organizations do allow ATVs and snowmobiles.

Trail descriptions themselves suggest an ideal itinerary for each route, including the best parking areas and access points, where to begin, your direction of travel, and any highlights along the way. The text notes any connecting or neighboring routes, with page numbers for the respective trail descriptions. Following each description are directions to the recommended trailheads.

Each trail description also lists a local website for further information. Be sure to visit these websites in advance for updates and current conditions. **TrailLink.com** is another great resource for updated content on the trails in this guidebook.

Trail Use

Rail-trails and multiuse trails are popular destinations for a range of users, often making them busy places to enjoy the outdoors. Following basic trail etiquette and safety guidelines will make your experience more pleasant.

➤ **Keep to the right,** except when passing.

➤ **Pass on the left,** and give a clear audible warning: "Passing on your left."

➤ **Be aware** of other trail users, particularly around corners and blind spots, and be especially careful when entering a trail, changing direction, or passing, so that you don't collide with traffic.

➤ **Respect wildlife** and public and private property; leave no trace and take out litter.

➤ **Control your speed,** especially near pedestrians, playgrounds, and heavily congested areas.

➤ **Travel single file.** Cyclists and pedestrians should ride or walk single file in congested areas or areas with reduced visibility.

➤ **Cross carefully** at intersections; always look both ways and yield to through traffic. Pedestrians have the right-of-way.

➤ **Keep one ear open and volume low** on portable listening devices to increase your awareness of your surroundings.

➤ **Wear a helmet** and other safety gear if you're cycling or in-line skating.

➤ **Consider visibility.** Wear reflective clothing, use bicycle lights, or bring flashlights or helmet-mounted lights for tunnel passages or twilight excursions.

➤ **Keep moving,** and don't block the trail. When taking a rest, turn off the trail to the right. Groups should avoid congregating on or blocking the trails. If you have an accident on the trail, move to the right as soon as possible.

➤ **Bicyclists yield** to all other trail users. Pedestrians yield to horses. If in doubt, yield to all other trail users.

➤ **Dogs are permitted on most trails,** but some trails through parks, wildlife refuges, or other sensitive areas may not allow pets; it's best to check the trail website before your visit. If pets are permitted, keep your dog on a short leash and under your control at all times. Remove dog waste in a designated trash receptacle.

➤ **Teach your children** these trail essentials, and be especially diligent to keep them out of faster-moving trail traffic.

➤ **Be prepared,** especially on long-distance rural trails. Bring water, snacks, maps, a light source, matches, and other equipment you may need. Because some areas may not have good reception for mobile phones, know where you're going, and tell someone else your plan.

Key to Trail Use

| cycling | in-line skating | fishing | wheel-chair access | horse-back riding | mountain biking | walking | cross-country skiing |

Learn More

While *Rail-Trails: Mid-Atlantic* is a helpful guide to available routes in the region, it wasn't feasible to list every rail-trail and multiuse trail in the Mid-Atlantic, and new trails spring up each year. To learn about additional multiuse trails in your area or to plan a trip to an area beyond the scope of this book, visit Rails-to-Trails Conservancy's trail-finder website, **TrailLink.com**—a free resource with information on more than 30,000 miles of trails nationwide.

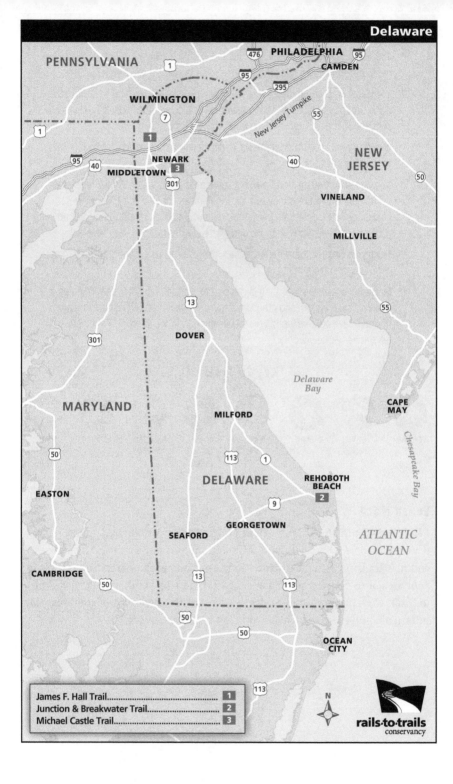

Delaware

PENNSYLVANIA

PHILADELPHIA
CAMDEN

WILMINGTON

NEW
JERSEY

NEWARK
MIDDLETOWN

VINELAND

MILLVILLE

DOVER

Delaware
Bay

MARYLAND

MILFORD

CAPE
MAY

DELAWARE

REHOBOTH
BEACH

Chesapeake Bay

EASTON

GEORGETOWN

ATLANTIC
OCEAN

SEAFORD

CAMBRIDGE

OCEAN
CITY

James F. Hall Trail.. 1
Junction & Breakwater Trail............................... 2
Michael Castle Trail.. 3

N

rails·to·trails
conservancy

Delaware

US 13 crosses over the Chesapeake and Delaware Canal along the Michael Castle Trail.

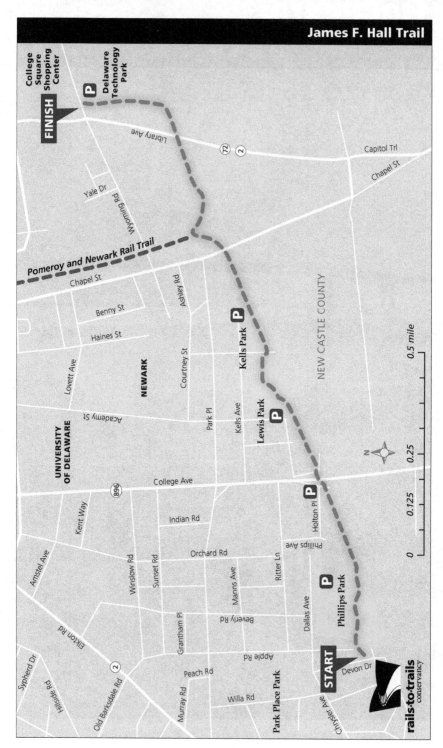

The James F. Hall Trail—a rail-with-trail—packs a lot into a short stretch: Its paved surface is great for bicycling, in-line skating, and strolling, and there are multiple playgrounds, picnic areas, and access points along the route. Best of all, this urban trail never crosses a road, so you can coast uninterrupted for its entire length from Phillips Park to Delaware Technology Park. The trail also offers alternative transportation benefits, connecting Newark neighborhoods with a regional transit station, the University of Delaware, and shopping centers.

Train aficionados are almost guaranteed to spot a train along the adjacent rail corridor, used by Amtrak, CSX, and the Southeastern Pennsylvania Transportation

A jogger heads east on the trail toward DE 72.

County
New Castle

Endpoints
Phillips Park to Delaware Technology Park at Wyoming Road (Newark)

Mileage
1.8

Type
Rail-with-Trail

Roughness Index
1

Surface
Asphalt

Authority (SEPTA). But you won't get too close to the trains because a large fence separates the trail from the active line. Families with young children will especially enjoy this route, which passes three city parks (Phillips, Lewis, and Kells) that feature swings, slides, baseball diamonds, and soccer fields, plus basketball, handball, and tennis courts. The trail also crosses streams and wetlands and runs through a semi-forested area. Police call boxes are provided every 0.1 mile, and the trail is lit for use after dark.

The James F. Hall Trail is also a connector trail, and just east of South Chapel Street, you can choose to head north on the 4.4-mile Pomeroy and Newark Rail Trail. That trail leads to White Clay Creek State Park, where it goes on to connect to the 2.3-mile Creek Road Trail.

CONTACT: cityofnewarkde.us

DIRECTIONS

To reach Bradford Ln. at the southeastern end of the trail, from I-95, take Exit 1 or 1B for DE 896 (College Ave.), and travel north 2.1 miles. Turn left onto W. Park Pl. After 0.4 mile, turn left onto Apple Road. After 0.3 mile, turn right onto Chrysler Ave. Follow Chrysler Ave. for 0.1 mile to Bradford Ln. (just after Devon Dr.). Turn left onto Bradford Ln. The trail is at the end of the road (0.2 mile). There is no dedicated parking at this location.

To reach the College Ave./SEPTA Station, from I-95, take Exit 1 or 1B for DE 896 (College Ave.), and travel north 1.6 miles to head downtown. Take a left onto Moplar St., and then take an immediate right to stay on Moplar. The SEPTA station and parking are to your right.

To reach Delaware Technology Park at the northern end of the trail, from I-95, take Exit 1 or 1B for DE 896 (College Ave.), and travel north 2.1 miles toward downtown. Turn right onto E. Park Pl., and take it for 0.6 mile. Turn left onto S. Chapel St. Turn right onto Wyoming Road, and take it for 0.6 mile. Park across from the College Square Shopping Center. The trail begins at the intersection of Wyoming Road and Library Ave.

This beautiful, pine-studded rail-trail winds through Cape Henlopen State Park next to wetlands and farmland, offering a break from the nearby beaches and eclectic shopping areas. The trail runs from Gills Neck Road in Lewes to the town of Rehoboth Beach and provides a perfect nature retreat.

The trail is mostly crushed stone, except for the last 0.2 mile near Rehoboth, when it becomes asphalt. As it is well traveled by locals and tourists alike, be sure to remember your trail etiquette. You will be sharing the mostly flat route with bicyclists, walkers, runners, wheelchair users, and families with strollers and dogs. Pick up the trail at Wolfe Glade (off Wolfe Neck Road), a forested area of oak, hemlock, and pine. Turn left to head 0.6 mile to the trail's beginning, or turn right to head toward Rehoboth Beach. You can also start at the western endpoint along Kings Highway/US 9 where it meets Gills Neck Road.

The cornfields, forests, and salt marshes of the region create a unique habitat for hawks.

County
Sussex

Endpoints
Kings Hwy./US 9 at Gills Neck Road (Lewes) to Hebron Road/CR 273 (Rehoboth)

Mileage
4.8

Type
Rail-Trail

Roughness Index
1

Surface
Asphalt, Crushed Stone

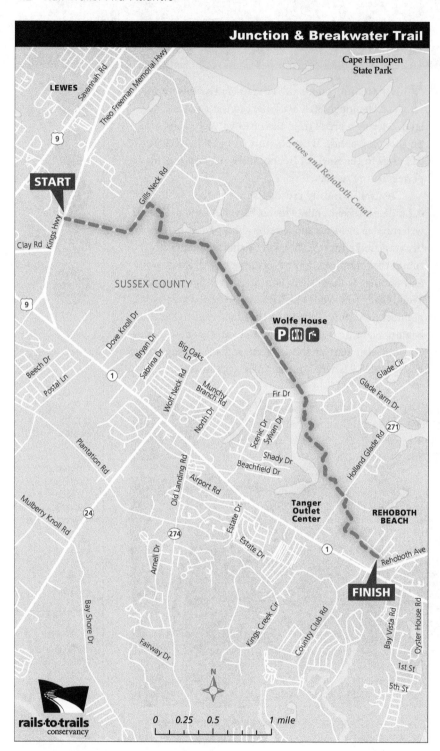

Junction & Breakwater Trail

Along the way, the trail offers views of wetlands—especially at Holland Glade—via a refurbished 80-foot railroad bridge built in 1913. Continue farther and you'll find yourself flanked by cornfields and forests. Hawks and geese (both snow and Canada geese) can be spotted in the air, and deer, squirrels, and other small woodland animals share the trail. At the trail's southern end, Tanger Outlets provides bargain hunters an opportunity to break from the trail, shop the mall, and grab a bite to eat before heading back into the relative calm of the Junction & Breakwater Trail.

CONTACT: **destateparks.com/activities/Trails/locations/cape-henlopen/#8**

DIRECTIONS

To reach the endpoint at Gills Neck Road, from the intersection of US 9, Bus. US 9, and DE 1, travel east on DE 1 for 1.2 miles, and then take a left onto Kings Hwy./Road 268. Go approximately 1 mile. The trail is on the right. There is no official parking at this trailhead.

To reach Wolfe Neck and parking, from the intersection of DE 1 and DE 1A in Dewey Beach, go 3.9 miles northwest on DE 1, and turn right onto Wolfe Neck Road. Go approximately 1 mile. You will see the Wolfe House on your right, where parking, restrooms, and a water fountain can be found next to the 0.2-mile path leading to the trail. (If you are traveling east on DE 1 from the intersection of US 9, Bus. US 9, and DE 1, you will go 3 miles, pass this turn, and make a U-turn at the next traffic light to access Wolfe Neck Road. You can also go slightly farther south on DE 1 and turn left onto Munchy Branch Road, which you follow 0.5 mile, where it turns left and goes another 0.7 mile until it hits Wolfe Neck Road.)

To reach the trail's end from the intersection of DE 1 and DE 1A in Dewey Beach, take DE 1 2.6 miles toward the Tanger Outlet Center (36470 Seaside Outlet Dr., Rehoboth Beach), which will be on your right. A bike/pedestrian path leads from the parking lot of the Tanger Outlet Center (look between the buildings in the middle) to the actual trail.

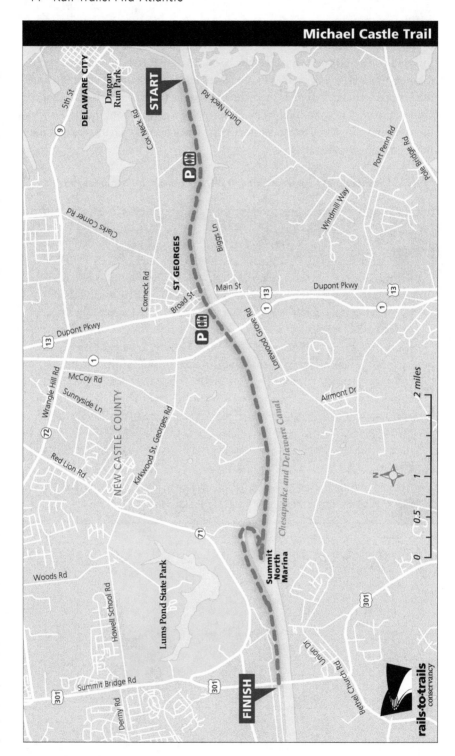

3 Michael Castle Trail

The Michael Castle Trail currently offers a scenic 9-mile route along the north shore of the Chesapeake and Delaware Canal in northern Delaware. The trail is named after the former governor and US representative whose efforts in Congress helped initiate the project on behalf of interested local trail users.

The C&D Canal opened in 1829, linking the Chesapeake Bay and Delaware River via a 14-mile route through what were once swampy marshlands. Today, the canal continues to be one of the world's busiest, as much of the shipping traffic to and from the Port of Baltimore—one of the largest ports in the United States—makes its way through the channel.

County
New Castle

Endpoints
Delaware City Branch Canal (south of Delaware City) to Summit Bridge (US 301/DE 896/DE 71) (Bear)

Mileage
8.7

Type
Greenway/Non-Rail-Trail

Roughness Index
1

Surface
Asphalt

A cyclist enjoys the solitude along the Chesapeake and Delaware Canal.

Starting at the eastern end of the trail just south of Delaware City, trail users can expect to see ships, and the paved trail accommodates such sightseeing with park benches lining the path. Along the route, the trail passes under three bridges, which serve as reminders of the canal's bisecting nature. Trail users looking for a more pastoral experience won't be disappointed, though: Native wildflowers, trees, and creatures of all sizes are also frequent sights.

The only diversion from the canal's edge is a brief arc around the Summit North Marina. (Note that horses are not permitted on this short section.) Just west of the boat slips, the trail emerges into the southern reaches of Lums Pond State Park, which surrounds the largest freshwater pond in the state. You can fish and boat, but not swim, in its waters, and several trails inside the park cater to hikers, bikers, horseback riders, and snowmobilers.

In the future, the Michael Castle Trail will be extended west from the Summit Bridge near Lums Pond State Park to quaint Chesapeake City, Maryland, near where the C&D Canal empties into the Chesapeake Bay. In the east, construction is under way on an extension to bring the trail into Delaware City, where it will provide easy access to both Fort DuPont State Park and an existing trail along the Branch Canal.

CONTACT: trails.delaware.gov

DIRECTIONS

On the eastern side of the trail, there are two trailheads with parking and restrooms: one in St. Georges under the US 13 bridge, and the other at Biddle Point off Cox Neck Road. To reach the St. Georges trailhead from I-95, take Exit 4 (DE 7/DE 1), and travel south on DE 1/DE 7 for 4.9 miles. Take Exit 156, and merge onto DE 1/US 13. Go 2.2 miles, and take Exit 152. Turn left onto DE 72/US 13, and after 0.3 mile, turn right onto US 13/DE 7. At 1.4 miles, take a slight right onto N. Main St. Continue 0.4 mile until N. Main St. reaches the Chesapeake and Delaware Canal and the trail.

To reach the Biddle Point trailhead, which also offers horse trailer parking, follow the directions above to Exit 152. Turn left onto DE 72/US 13, and after 0.3 mile, turn right onto US 13/DE 7. At 1 mile, turn left onto Cox Neck Road. After 1.6 miles, turn right at a sign for the C&D Canal Wildlife Area. Follow the road 0.6 mile to the Chesapeake and Delaware Canal and the trail.

To reach the Summit Bridge trailhead (just south of Lums Pond State Park), from Middletown, at the intersection of US 301 and DE 299, take US 301 north for 8.5 miles. Turn right onto DE 71, and go 0.8 mile. Turn right onto Old Summit Road, and go 0.4 mile. A small gravel lot will be on your right. Or from Exit 1 or 1A on I-95, merge onto DE 896 (S. College Ave.) south toward Middletown. After 6.1 miles, turn left onto DE 71, and follow the directions above.

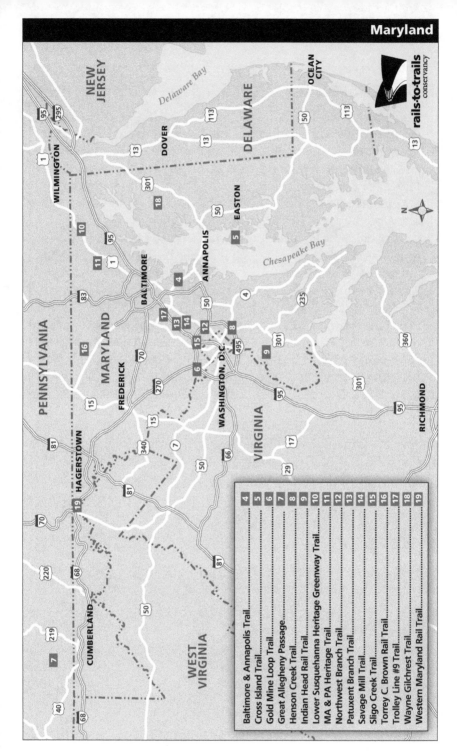

Maryland

rails-to-trails conservancy

4	Baltimore & Annapolis Trail
5	Cross Island Trail
6	Gold Mine Loop Trail
7	Great Allegheny Passage
8	Henson Creek Trail
9	Indian Head Rail Trail
10	Lower Susquehanna Heritage Greenway Trail
11	MA & PA Heritage Trail
12	Northwest Branch Trail
13	Patuxent Branch Trail
14	Savage Mill Trail
15	Sligo Creek Trail
16	Torrey C. Brown Rail Trail
17	Trolley Line #9 Trail
18	Wayne Gilchrest Trail
19	Western Maryland Rail Trail

Maryland

For history buffs, the community of Chestertown and the Wayne Gilchrest Trail are must-visit destinations.

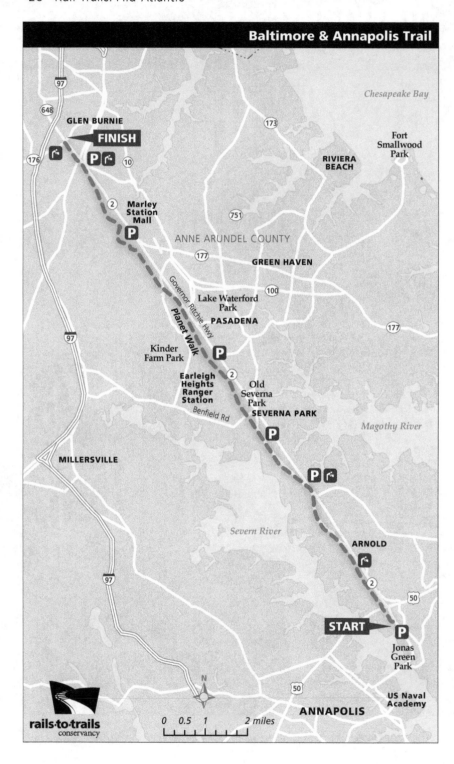

Baltimore & Annapolis Trail

Chesapeake Bay

97

648

GLEN BURNIE

173

176

10

Fort
Smallwood
Park

RIVIERA
BEACH

2 Marley
Station
Mall

751

ANNE ARUNDEL COUNTY

177

GREEN HAVEN

Governor Ritchie Hwy

Lake Waterford
Park

100

Planet Walk

PASADENA

177

Kinder
Farm Park

Earleigh
Heights
Ranger
Station

Benfield Rd

2

Old
Severna
Park

SEVERNA PARK

Magothy River

MILLERSVILLE

97

Severn River

ARNOLD

2

50

START

Jonas
Green
Park

97

N

50

US Naval
Academy

ANNAPOLIS

rails·to·trails
conservancy

0   0.5   1   2 miles

4 Baltimore & Annapolis Trail

If you wish to augment your physical workout with some intellectual exercise, look no farther than the Baltimore & Annapolis Trail. The scenic, paved, 13.3-mile community trail is brimming with history lessons and boasts a solar system of information. The trail follows the route of the Annapolis & Baltimore Short Line, which started running freight and passenger service in 1887 and helped shape this suburban region near the nation's capital. Today, the 112-acre linear park winds through parks, neighborhoods, and natural wooded areas.

The route passes the Marley Station shopping mall, for those looking for some retail therapy to accompany their trek. History buffs might want to stop in at the Earleigh Heights Ranger Station, circa 1889. The trail features several pocket parks along the way—charming, landscaped

County
Anne Arundel

Endpoints
Jonas Green Park (Annapolis) to Dorsey Road (Glen Burnie)

Mileage
13.3

Type
Rail-Trail

Roughness Index
1

Surface
Asphalt

Interesting art along the trail provides a good excuse for a short break.

nooks with picnic tables and an open invitation to rest your feet for a spell. One such setting is Olde Severna Park, near the Park Plaza Shopping Center (intersection of Baltimore Annapolis Boulevard and West McKinsey Road), where local bike shop Pedal Pushers caters to trail riders with rentals—and the local pizza and frozen yogurt shops adjacent appeal to hungry passersby. The B&A takes its beautification seriously. Portions of the route are sponsored by volunteers who fill the flower beds and kiosks along the trail, lending it a colorful, seasonal flair.

Along the trail, you will find a literal alphabet of historical markers, from A to Z. The A marker, at mile 0.1, is the Winchester Station House at Manresa, near the Annapolis start of the trail. At mile 13.3, you will find the Z marker, identifying the Sawmill Branch, the area's source of water and power in the early 18th century. To follow along with each marker, pick up a flier at the ranger station.

From the ranger station to Harundale Plaza, you will stroll or bike beside the Planet Walk, a linear museum with informative displays for the sun and each planet. The planets are true to scale and feature storyboards that teach about our solar system. The trail, and its educational opportunities, ends in the small town of Glen Burnie. But you may continue on the BWI Trail loop for an additional 12.5 miles around the Baltimore Washington International Airport.

CONTACT: aacounty.org/recparks/parks/trails/bandatrailpark.cfm or
dnr.state.md.us/greenways/ba_trail.html

DIRECTIONS

The Annapolis trailhead is located off US 50 past the Severn River. Take Exit 27 and head south less than 0.25 mile toward the U.S. Naval Academy on MD 450. The parking lot for Jonas Green Park is on the right. Directions to the trail via an on-road bike lane are on the board near the entrance of the parking lot. The actual rail-trail begins at Boulters Way.

To reach the Glen Burnie trailhead, take US 50 east from Washington, D.C., to Exit 21, and follow I-97 north 42 miles. Take Exit 15 leading to MD 176 E/Dorsey Road. Continue on MD 176 for approximately 0.6 mile before turning right onto MD 648/Baltimore and Annapolis Blvd. At the first light (after 0.5 mile), take a right onto Crain Hwy. and then a right onto Central Ave. The parking lot is on the right and runs along the trail.

Maryland's Cross Island Trail spans Kent Island, east to west, in Queen Anne's County, providing multiple points of access to everything from libraries and schools to ball fields and the waterfront. It's an impressively signed, well-maintained, charming trail with some truly exceptional views.

Begin at Terrapin Nature Park, a parcel of protected land for birds and native plant life. Just past the nature area, to the left of the trail, is an old graveyard with fewer than a dozen cracked and weathered headstones tucked among the trees. If you can spot it, it's worth a peek. From

County
Queen Anne's

Endpoints
Terrapin Nature Park to Kent Narrows (Kent Island)

Mileage
6

Type
Rail-Trail

Roughness Index
1

Surface
Asphalt

Get a taste of Chesapeake Bay on the Cross Island Trail.

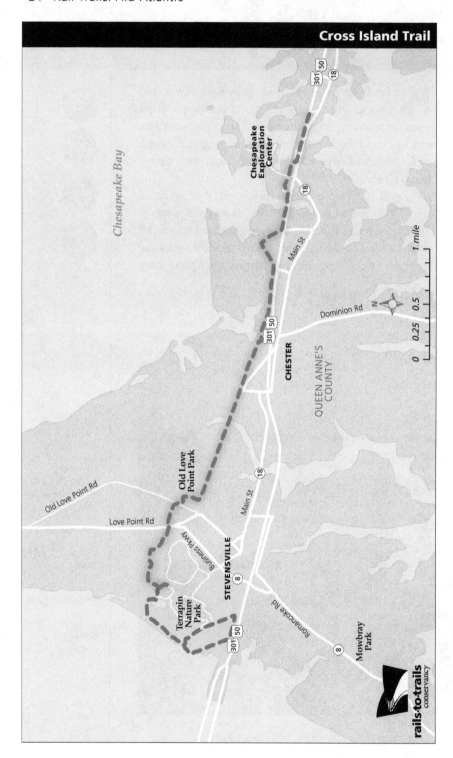

Cross Island Trail

Chesapeake Bay

Chesapeake Exploration Center

Main St

301 50 18

18

Dominion Rd

1 mile

0.5

0.25

0

N

301 50

CHESTER

QUEEN ANNE'S COUNTY

Old Love Point Park

Old Love Point Rd

Love Point Rd

Business Pkwy

Main St

18

STEVENSVILLE

8

Terrapin Nature Park

301 50

Romancoke Rd

8

Mowbray Park

rails-to-trails
conservancy

here, the trail quickly winds through neighborhoods and stands of white pines and hemlocks. At the first mile marker, you come to Old Love Point Park, a recreation area with baseball and soccer fields.

Continuing along, the trail passes through farmlands, and you'll be able to see a lighthouse in the distance that indicates how close you really are to the seashore. At mile 3.8, you will have to do a short back-road jog to reconnect with the trail, but a blue-painted bike lane makes this a simple transition. Back on the path, you'll come to a long wooden bridge that provides the first unhindered view of the water. This lovely expanse is a gem on the Cross Island Trail.

To access the Chesapeake Exploration Center in Kent Narrows, head left onto Piney Narrows Road, which bends right toward the water. The center is located at the end of the road, to the left.

Or to continue along the trail, when you reach the marina, head uphill to cross over the causeway, MD 18/Main Street, where there is an extremely wide shoulder. Here, the trail becomes a series of sidewalks and access points to the waterfront and its restaurants and boat slips.

CONTACT: parksnrec.org

DIRECTIONS

To reach the start at Terrapin Nature Park, from Annapolis, take US 50 east to Exit 37 (the first exit after crossing the Chesapeake Bay Bridge). After 0.3 mile, turn left onto MD 8. Follow MD 8 0.4 mile to the Chesapeake Bay Business Park, and turn left. Follow the road to the right around the circle until you come to Terrapin Nature Park. There is ample parking, and portable toilets are at the trailhead. Note that you must purchase and display a Queen Anne's County Beach Permit to leave your vehicle in the park's parking lot.

To reach Kent Narrows, take US 50 east from Annapolis. Take Exit 41/MD 18 E/Main St. Follow MD 18 for just under 1 mile (you'll pass over Kent Narrows on a bridge), and then turn left onto Kent Narrows Road. Turn left onto Narrows Road. Parking is available under the bridge.

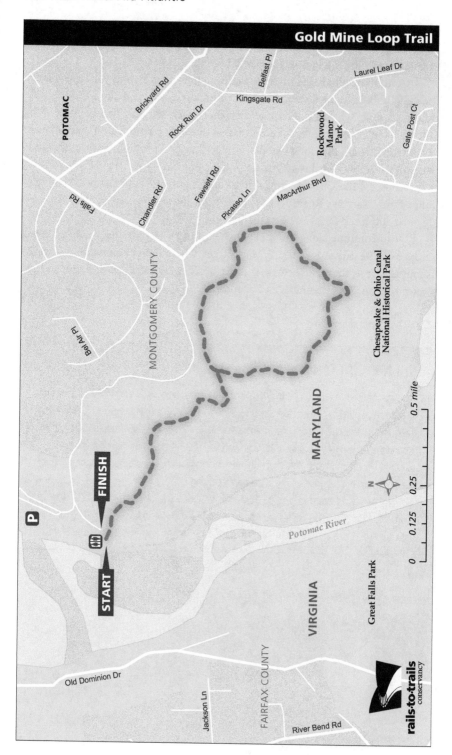

6 Gold Mine Loop Trail

Tucked in the meandering, wooded hills of the sprawling yet understated multimillion-dollar estates of Great Falls, just outside Washington, D.C., is the Chesapeake & Ohio Canal National Historical Park. Home to the already famous C&O Canal Towpath, the Great Falls section of the park also hosts this unique rail-trail circuit.

The trail begins at the hillside just beyond the historic, early 1800s Great Falls Tavern Visitor Center. Start at the well-marked post and head up a series of stairs that are cut into the hillside and reinforced with logs. This is not your traditional rail-trail. Only part of it runs on the former railroad corridor, so prepare for some gentle uphill climbs. (The trail is off-limits to bicycles.)

The path, marked by a blue blaze, immediately takes you into the surrounding airy forest. After less than a mile, you reach the beginning of the actual loop. Take note: Detours on yellow-blazed spur trails along the route take you to the Maryland Mine ruins, where gold was

Even little ones enjoy exploring the woodlands along this route.

County
Montgomery

Endpoints
Great Falls Tavern Visitor Center (Potomac)

Mileage
2.5

Type
Rail-Trail

Roughness Index
2

Surface
Dirt

processed from 1867 to 1939. Upon reaching the start of the loop, go either left or right; both ways will take you back to this starting point.

If you head to the right, you will first come to the Woodland Trail Spur (one of six trail spurs along the loop), where you'll cross a tiny creek and the surface will change from dirt to gravel. If you are on the trail in the spring, several stands of redbud will be blooming, providing a vibrant color contrast to the grayish-green of an awakening forest. At certain points, you may have to scramble over, under, or around impressive felled trees, but they only add to the trail's woodland feel.

When you return to the beginning of the loop, take the path back to the visitor center and explore the rest of the park. Don't miss the nearby Great Falls overlook, which provides stunning views of the waterfall that separates the upper and lower Potomac River. Pick up a trail map at the ranger station to find directions to the overlook.

CONTACT: nps.gov/grfa

DIRECTIONS

From the Capital Beltway/I-495, take Exit 41 (Carderock/Great Falls), and follow Clara Barton Pkwy. west for 1.7 miles. At the stop sign (at the end of the road), make a slight left onto MacArthur Blvd. Go 3.5 miles to the end of the road at the park. There is an entry fee.

Near Great Falls, this 2.5-mile loop offers something unique for hikers and equestrians.

7 Great Allegheny Passage

N ow the longest rail-trail east of the Mississippi River, the 150-mile Great Allegheny Passage (GAP) spans two states in its course along great rivers and across mountain passes. Running from Pittsburgh, Pennsylvania, to Cumberland, Maryland, the route traces the paths of railroads that helped build America.

Beginning in Pittsburgh's Point State Park, the trail overlaps the Eliza Furnace segment of the Three Rivers Heritage Trail. An array of signage interprets the area's industrial past. The Hot Metal Bridge, once used to carry iron by rail from the Eliza Furnace to Pittsburgh's South Side to produce finished steel, leads trail users across the Monongahela River to the Three Rivers Heritage Trail's South Side and Baldwin Borough segments, which extend south to Homestead.

Counties
Allegany, Allegheny (PA), Fayette (PA), Somerset (PA), Westmoreland (PA)

Endpoints
Point State Park near Commonwealth Pl. and Liberty Ave. (Pittsburgh, PA) to Western Maryland Railway Station at Canal St. (Cumberland, MD)

Mileage
150

Type
Rail-Trail

Roughness Index
1

Surface
Asphalt, Crushed Stone

Cyclists flock to this scenic, shady pathway.

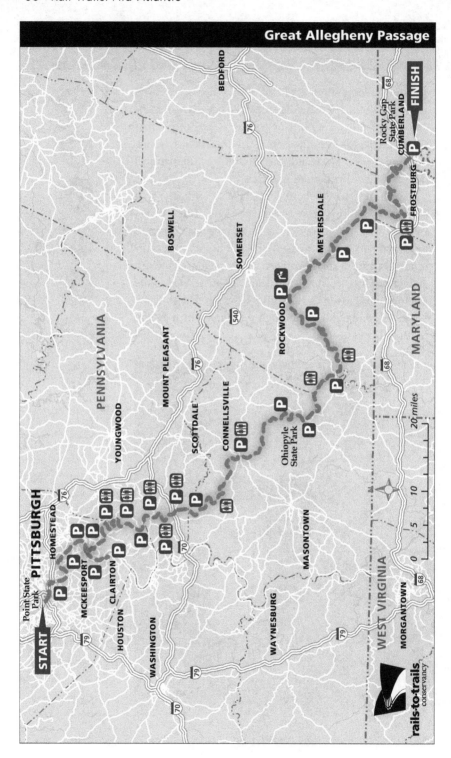

In the small Pittsburgh suburb, massive industrial furnaces from the Homestead Steel Works stand along with smaller artifacts, such as a ladle car. These industrial artifacts and interpretive signage add interest to both the trail and The Waterfront, a modern retail center with offices, restaurants, and entertainment, all rebuilt to reflect early 20th-century charm and its industrial past.

The Great Allegheny Passage heads south from Homestead to McKeesport through former steel mill sites along the banks of the Monongahela River. Here, the GAP splits into two, with the on-road Clairton Connector heading west through Glassport to meet the Montour Trail in Clairton, and the main trail continuing south along the former route of the Pittsburgh, McKeesport and Youghiogheny Railroad.

Built in 1883, the railroad carried coal and coke from the rich town of Connellsville to the Pittsburgh steel mills. Nicknamed the P-Mickey for its initials (P., McK., and Y.), it eventually merged with the Pittsburgh & Lake Erie Railroad. The freight and coal traffic that sustained the branch dried up by the mid-1980s, and the line fell into disuse in 1990.

As you travel south along the Youghiogheny River from McKeesport, you pass lush green hillsides and once-booming industrial towns. The first 40 miles of this segment go through the Pennsylvania towns of Boston, West Newton, and Dawson. Trailside B&Bs, bike shops, and cafés welcome trail users in these towns, making them great resting spots.

Eventually, the Great Allegheny Passage reaches the historic boomtown of Connellsville, where the industrial revolution is still alive. This self-proclaimed trail town offers wonderful parks, restaurants, and cafés. Near South Connellsville, hikers and bikers can hop on the short Sheepskin Trail to travel southwest to the tiny community of Dunbar.

For the next 28 miles, the Great Allegheny Passage follows the Youghiogheny River through Ohiopyle State Park. Take refuge under the dense canopy of the hardwood forest on the river's edge. Before reaching the quaint town of Ohiopyle, you cross two impressive trestles. The town is a home base for adventure seekers. The trail is a central attraction, but the wild and untamed Youghiogheny River here makes it a popular whitewater-rafting destination as well.

The trail continues south along the river to Confluence. Aptly named, the town is built where the Youghiogheny River, Casselman River, and Laurel Hill Creek come together. It has plenty of great places to eat or get a good night's rest.

South of Confluence, the trail leaves the Youghiogheny and heads northeast for 31 miles, following the Casselman River to Meyersdale. You bypass the 849-foot-long Pinkerton Tunnel along this stretch. This segment also features the Salisbury Viaduct, 1,908 feet long and more than 100 feet at its highest point, which you'll cross shortly before reaching Meyersdale. The town offers a pleasant old trailside train depot that provides good local information.

You continue a gentle climb as the path heads southeast toward the Eastern Continental Divide. Here, the trail follows the route of the old Western Maryland Railroad, which began operations between Cumberland, Maryland, and Connellsville, Pennsylvania, in 1912. Sold to a competitor in 1931, the railroad was operational for many more years before falling into disuse. The Keystone Viaduct, a 910-foot-long bridge, can be found along this gorgeous part of the trail.

You cross the Eastern Continental Divide just before reaching the Maryland state line. From this elevation of 2,400 feet, it's all downhill to Cumberland. Pass through the 0.5-mile-long Big Savage Tunnel just beyond the divide, and take in stunning views of the surrounding hills and agricultural valleys as you pass the Mason-Dixon Line into Maryland, just beyond the tunnel. Frostburg is the first town you reach, about 5 miles into Maryland. The city features a restored passenger and freight station—now open as a restaurant—originally built in 1891.

The trail leaves Frostburg and continues another 16 miles through rolling Maryland countryside to Cumberland. For much of this section, the route parallels the active Western Maryland Scenic Railroad, and you may catch glimpses of its steam locomotive. The popular excursion line provides scenic three-hour trips through the Allegheny Mountains.

Cumberland, the terminus of the Great Allegheny Passage, does not disappoint. A pedestrian mall downtown has many restaurants and shops. In Cumberland, the trail connects to the Chesapeake & Ohio Canal National Historical Park towpath (also known as the C&O Canal Towpath), which takes you another 184 miles to Washington, D.C., without ever leaving a trail.

Note that equestrians are permitted only on the grassy areas of the Great Allegheny Passage between Boston and Connellsville, Pennsylvania; Rockwood and Garrett, Pennsylvania; and the Maryland–Pennsylvania state line and Frostburg, Maryland. Before you set out on a long journey to explore the trail, check **atatrail.org** for updates on detours and other safety information.

CONTACT: atatrail.org

DIRECTIONS

Some of the best parking for the Great Allegheny Passage can be found south of Pittsburgh along Waterfront Dr. in the shopping area in Homestead. Take I-376 to Exit 74. Travel south on Beechwood Blvd., which turns into Browns Hill Road, for 1.2 miles. Cross the Homestead Grays Bridge, and take the first right onto Fifth Ave. After 0.4 mile, turn right onto Waterfront Dr. The shopping area will be on your right; the trail parallels Waterfront Dr. on your left.

To reach the McKeesport trailhead farther south, take PA 837 out of Pittsburgh and follow signs to McKeesport (about 13 miles south of downtown). Cross the McKeesport–Duquesne Bridge and pick up PA 148/Lysle Blvd. going right (west) toward McKeesport. Follow the road about 1.2 miles into town, and veer onto the Water St. ramp on your right. Take a left onto Water St.; parking is located at Richard J. Gergely Riverfront Park.

Parking can also be found near where the Great Allegheny Passage and Montour Trail meet just off PA 837 in Clairton, off N. State St.

Free parking is available at the trailheads in Confluence, Ohiopyle, Connellsville, Meyersdale, Garrett, Rockwood, Markleton, and Fort Hill as well.

From Pittsburgh to the access point in Frostburg, take I-76 to Exit 110. Continue on N. Pleasant Ave. for 0.9 mile. Turn left onto E. Main St., and after 0.3 mile, take a slight right onto Berlin Plank Road/US 219/Flight 93 Memorial Hwy. After 8.1 miles, continue on Broadway St. for 0.3 mile, and turn left onto Main St. After 0.4 mile, turn right onto PA 160 S/Cumberland St. Continue on this road for 11.9 miles; then turn right onto PA 2011/McKenzie Hollow Road. Travel 4.1 miles, and turn left onto Greenville Road, which turns into MD 546. After 3 miles, turn left onto MD 946 S. Follow this for 0.6 mile, and turn left onto Alt. US 40 E/National Pike. Continue for 3.4 miles, and turn left onto Depot Terrace, which intersects with Depot St. in less than 0.5 mile. Take a left, and the trail (and New Hope Road) will be immediately on your right. Another parking area is available 0.2 mile down New Hope Road just north of Rankin Dr.

To reach the Cumberland trailhead in Maryland from I-68, take Exit 43B. Upon exiting, take a left onto W. Harrison St. and then an immediate right onto S. Mechanic St. The old Western Maryland train depot on your left has public parking for the trail.

Visit **atatrail.org** for more information about the many other access points along the Great Allegheny Passage.

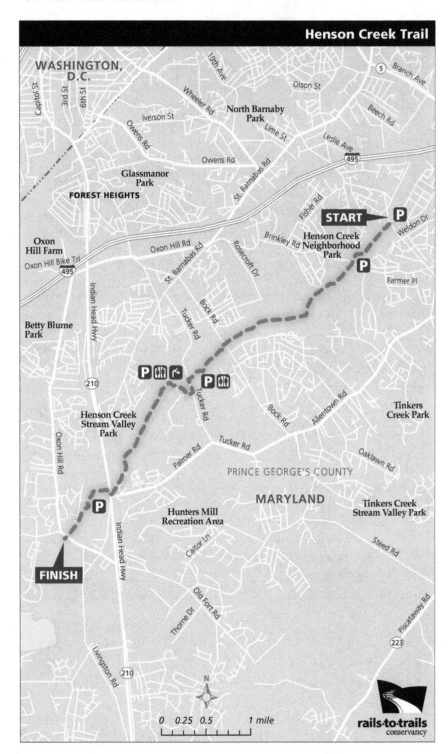

8 Henson Creek Trail

The Henson Creek Trail is located in the southwestern portion of Prince George's County, Maryland, and connects the growing District of Columbia suburbs of Fort Washington and Oxon Hill with the bedroom communities of Camp Springs and Temple Hills. The trail follows the course of Henson Creek for its entire route.

Extending from Temple Hill Road southward to Oxon Hill Road, the trail passes through Henson Creek Neighborhood Park; crosses Brinkley Road through the Henson Creek Stream Valley Park; passes Rosecroft Raceway, a historic harness racing track; and winds through

Follow Henson Creek as it winds through Prince George's County.

County
Prince George's

Endpoints
Temple Hill Road and Henderson Road (Camp Springs) to Oxon Hill Road and Fort Foote Road (Fort Washington)

Mileage
5.7

Type
Greenway/Non-Rail-Trail

Roughness Index
1

Surface
Asphalt

a number of residential neighborhoods. Heading south into the Tucker Road Ice Rink and Athletic Complex parking lot, turn south onto Tucker Road for a brief jog before turning west onto Ferguson Lane at the Tucker Road Community Center. Make an immediate right to pick up Henson Creek Trail again and reunite with the creek path.

After crossing under busy Indian Head Highway/MD 210, the Henson Creek Trail reaches its southern terminus at Oxon Hill Road (located about 1 mile south of the new National Harbor development). A grassy shoulder immediately adjacent to the paved trail accommodates equestrian users for the entire length of the greenway, but beware: Erosion is affecting portions of the route, and caution should be exercised at all times.

CONTACT: pgparks.com/Your_Parks/Trails/Henson_Creek_Trail.htm

DIRECTIONS

Parking for the Henson Creek Trail can be found at its northern endpoint in Temple Hills Park off Temple Hill Road (just south of Henderson Road). From the Capital Beltway/I-495, take Exit 7A (Branch Ave. S/MD 5) toward Waldorf. Follow MD 5 for 1.5 miles to the Allentown Road exit (MD 337), and bear right onto Allentown Road toward Camp Springs. In less than 0.5 mile, turn right onto Brinkley Road. Go approximately 1 mile, and turn right onto Temple Hill Road. Follow it approximately 1 mile to Temple Hills Park on the right.

The large athletic complex on Tucker Road north of Ferguson Ln. also contains a parking lot with ample space. Take the Capital Beltway/I-495 to Exit 4A (St. Barnabas Road/MD 414), and keep left at the fork. Turn right to stay on St. Barnabas Road; after 0.8 mile, turn left onto Tucker Road. The athletic complex will be on your left after a little more than 1 mile.

9 Indian Head Rail Trail

L
ocated just 18 miles south of our nation's capital, the Indian Head Rail Trail offers a unique natural outdoor experience, seemingly far removed from urban development and its associated chaotic pace. The trail was a generous gift of a former railroad corridor from the National Park Service's Federal Lands to Parks Program. The line was built in 1918 to transport supplies for the U.S. Navy's Indian Head Powder Factory, founded 28 years earlier as the U.S. Navy's first established presence in southern Maryland.

The 13-mile, paved Indian Head Rail Trail traverses roughly halfway across Charles County, connecting the small towns of Indian Head and White Plains. Cyclists and hikers can experience the surroundings of mature forests,

See remnants of the trail's railroad past along the way.

County
Charles

Endpoints
Mattingly Ave. near Naval Station (Indian Head) to Theodore Green Blvd. west of US 301 (White Plains)

Mileage
13.4

Type
Rail-Trail

Roughness Index
1

Surface
Asphalt

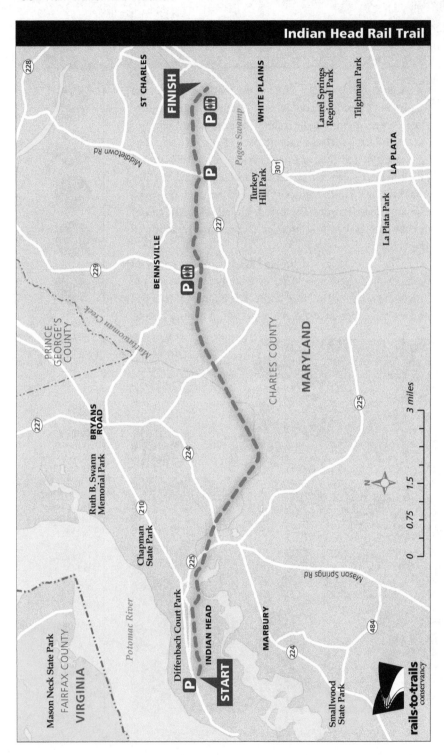

Indian Head Rail Trail

natural wetlands, and occasional farmland as they pass through the Mattawoman Creek stream valley and some of southern Maryland's most scenic and undeveloped natural areas.

Notable wildlife sightings include wild turkey, deer, herons, bald eagles, egrets, and a variety of waterfowl. Leaving Indian Head, approximately 2 miles out, visitors will encounter a spectacular view of the backwaters of Mattawoman Creek as it winds on its course toward the Potomac River. As with any trail that shares such close proximity with a waterway, you'll pass over numerous bridges. Just be sure you don't miss the many interpretative signs along the way; take the time to learn more of the region's history. Or simply kick back on the trailside benches and soak in the scenery. No matter your pace, the Indian Head Rail Trail is bound to delight.

CONTACT: dnr.state.md.us/greenways/counties/princegeorges.html

DIRECTIONS

There is no parking at the Mattingly Ave. trailhead in Indian Head, but ample parking is located across MD 210 at either the Village Green Town Park or Charlie Wright Park (101 Dr. Mitchell Ln.). To access this parking lot, from Fort Washington, take Indian Head Hwy./MD 210 S for approximately 13 miles. Turn right onto Lackey Dr., and at the end of the road, turn left onto Dr. Mitchell Ln.

Parking is also available at Bensville Park off Bensville Road/MD 229 south of Bensville. From Fort Washington, take Indian Head Hwy./MD 210 S approximately 4 miles, and turn left onto MD 228. After 1.5 miles, take a right onto Bensville Road. Bensville Park is 4.3 miles down on the left.

Another access point is on Middletown Road north of Marshall Corner Road. To get to this lot, follow the directions above to MD 228, but continue on MD 228 for 3.8 miles and turn right onto Middletown Road. Continue for 4 miles, and the lot will be on your left.

Parking is also available at the southeastern terminus off Theodore Green Blvd. in White Plains. To reach it, follow the directions above, but bypass Middletown Road. Follow MD 228 its entire length, 6.8 miles, and then turn right onto US 301. Continue on US 301 for 3.3 miles to reach Theodore Green Blvd. on your right.

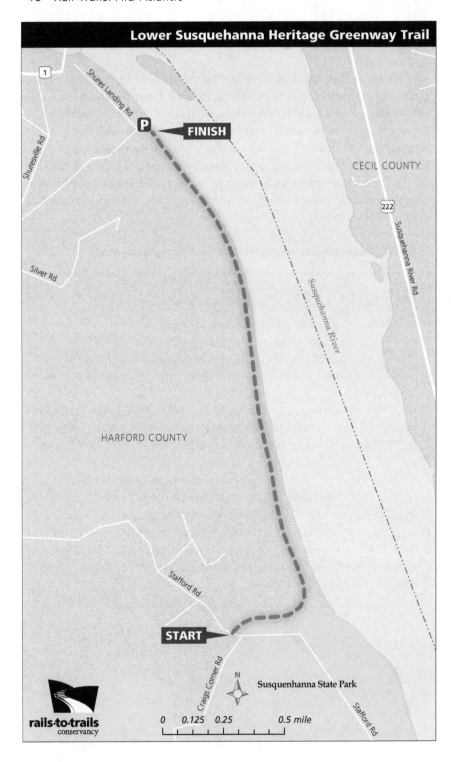

10 Lower Susquehanna Heritage Greenway Trail

Maryland's Susquehanna State Park is recognized for challenging hiking and biking trails, camping facilities, rock outcrops, boating, a museum, and restored historical sites. But none of these outshines the Susquehanna River, which sweeps majestically by, beckoning fishermen and nature lovers.

Take in the scenic river by venturing out on the Lower Susquehanna Heritage Greenway Trail along the western bank. The Philadelphia Electric Company built the corridor in 1926 to transport materials from Havre d'Grace on the Chesapeake Bay to the construction site of the Conowingo

Counties
Cecil, Harford

Endpoints
Shures Landing Road (Conowingo Dam) to Stafford Road (Susquehanna State Park)

Mileage
2.5

Type
Rail-Trail

Roughness Index
1

Surface
Crushed Stone

The wide, stone-dust path adjacent to the Susquehanna River is easy to walk or bike.

Dam. The dam was completed in two years, and the rail line, no longer needed, became a victim of overgrowth and erosion until the Lower Susquehanna Heritage Greenway Trail was created.

Eventually, it will extend 50 miles along both sides of the river; presently, only 2.5 miles are open. To start the trail from the south, in Susquehanna State Park, go to the north side of the Deer Creek bridge. Near this end, where the trail travels inland to the sparkling Deer Creek, is the site of the early Stafford flint furnace, with a portion of the furnace still standing. Along the way to the impressive 4,648-foot-long, 102-foot-high Conowingo Dam, you'll pass wooded wetlands harboring songbirds and abundant wildflowers, especially in the spring. You may also spot old rail tracks and informational displays with historical and scientific details about the area.

The wide, stone-dust trail is easy to walk or bike, and though a dense canopy overhead offers shade in the summer months, the river views are frequent and beautiful. Near the northern end, a viewing platform provides river access to anglers, bird-watchers (the dam is a feeding ground for many varieties), and others.

CONTACT: **dnr2.maryland.gov/publiclands/Pages/central/susquehanna.aspx**

DIRECTIONS

To start from the south, take Exit 89 from I-95. Follow MD 155 south, and take the first left onto Lapidum Road. After 2.4 miles, turn left onto Stafford Road, and follow it 1.3 miles to Susquehanna State Park and the Deer Creek picnic area on the north end.

To reach the northern trailhead, take I-95 north from Baltimore to Exit 85. Follow MD 22 north 4.2 miles to MD 136/Priestford Road, continuing north for 5.6 miles. Upon reaching US 1/ Conowingo Road, go north (right). After 5.3 miles, turn right onto Shuresville Road and then, in 0.7 mile, left onto Shures Landing Road. Follow this 1.1 miles to Conowingo Dam, and look for the trailhead just south of the dam at Fisherman's Park.

11 MA & PA Heritage Trail

The MA & PA Heritage Trail is composed of two segments (about 2 miles apart) through the wooded parks of the Bel Air and Forest Hill communities. The folksy-sounding name actually stands for the Maryland and Pennsylvania Railroad, which screamed through the Harford County countryside, heralding industrial progress of the early 1900s.

Today, a new kind of progress is evident in the sound of twittering birds and babbling brooks on the long-deserted rail line. This refreshing natural oasis found on the MA & PA Heritage Trail lures visitors as well as residents of the neighborhoods just steps from the path.

If you plan to travel both portions, follow the directions below between the two segments. Both have ample parking and are easy to navigate, with a surface of stone dust; the Bel Air portion also has some paving on slopes.

Families (and dogs) enjoy the MA & PA Heritage Trail.

County
Harford

Endpoints
Williams St. at Ellendale St. to Edgeley Grove (Bel Air) and Jarrettsville Road to Melrose Ln. (Forest Hill)

Mileage
5

Type
Rail-Trail

Roughness Index
1

Surface
Crushed Stone, Dirt

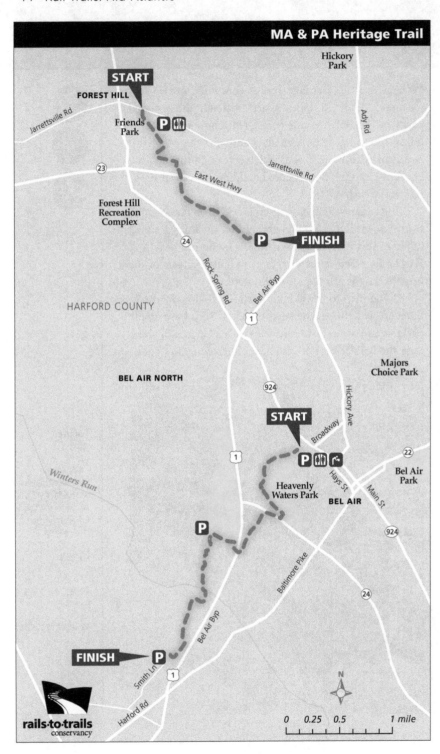

MA & PA Heritage Trail

The southern segment, starting in Bel Air, weaves through old stands of native trees, rising and falling with the dips of the landscape. For 3.3 miles, it travels past streams, over bridges, through a tunnel, and across a boardwalk section between Heavenly Waters Park and Edgeley Grove Farm at Annie's Playground. This lovely green space provides a protected natural environment and a perfect setting for a stroll or jog.

From Forest Hill in the northern segment, the rail-trail meanders for 1.7 miles between Friends Park off Jarrettsville Road and Blake's Venture Park near Bynum Road and Melrose Lane. The trail passes among the forest, past an enchanting marsh teeming with wildlife, and through tidy developments of suburban homes, a light industrial area, and recreational ball fields.

North or south, the community parks framing the endpoints of the MA & PA Heritage Trail beckon you to slow down, enjoy a picnic, or watch the sun go down.

CONTACT: **mapatrail.org**

DIRECTIONS

To reach the northern endpoint of the Bel Air section from I-95, take MD 24 (Exit 77B) north toward Bel Air. Turn right onto Baltimore Pike/Bus. US 1; after 0.3 mile, turn left onto Atwood St. After 0.5 mile, turn right onto Catherine St. Make a left onto Williams St. Go 0.3 mile; the trail parking lot is on the left.

To reach the parking lot at the southern endpoint, located at Edgeley Grove and Annie's Playground, take Exit 74 (MD 152/Mountain Road) from I-95. Follow MD 152 north toward Fallston for 5 miles, and turn right onto MD 147/Harford Road. After 0.8 mile, turn left onto Connolly Road and make an immediate right onto Smith Ln. The lot is located about 0.5 mile farther.

To access the northern endpoint of the Forest Hill segment, take Exit 77 (MD 24) off I-95. Follow MD 24 north 6.4 miles, and take a right onto US 1. After 1.6 miles, exit US 1 and follow Rock Spring Road/MD 24 north for about 2.5 miles. Turn right onto E. Jarrettsville Road, and then take an immediate right into Friends Park. Follow the drive past the pond and up the rise to the trailhead. To reach the Melrose Ln. endpoint, take US 1 to Rock Spring Road/MD 24, and make the first right onto Bynum Road. Where Bynum curves east, at 0.7 mile, turn left onto Melrose Ln., and then turn left again into the parking area just a few hundred yards farther.

If you plan on completing both portions of the trail, follow these directions from the northern Bel Air endpoint to Friends Park in Forest Hills. Turn left (north) onto Rock Spring Road/MD 24, and go 3.6 miles to E. Jarrettsville Road. Turn right and travel 0.2 mile. Friends Park is on your right.

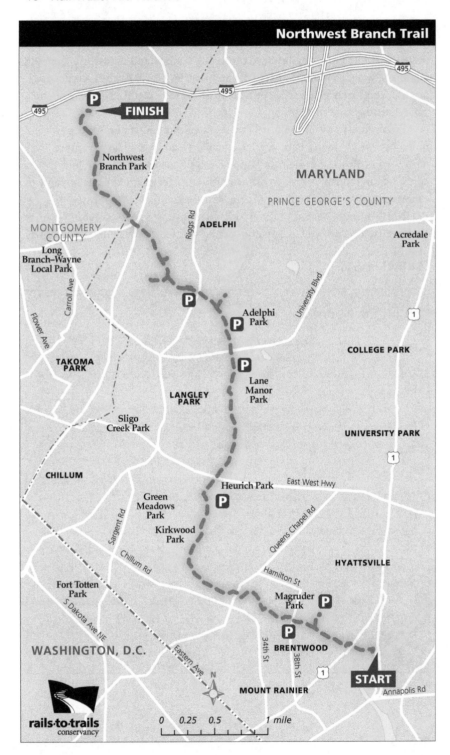

Northwest Branch Trail

12 Northwest Branch Trail

The Northwest Branch Trail—an integral part of the Anacostia Tributary Trail System—runs between Hyattsville and Silver Spring, linking two bustling suburbs of Washington, D.C. The trail is so named because it follows the Northwest Branch of the Anacostia River for its entire route.

The trail begins in the south in Prince George's County, just north of where the river splits into its northeast and northwest branches. Appropriately, direct connections to the Northeast Branch Trail and Anacostia River Trail can be found here. North of this trail hub, the Northwest Branch Trail runs past a succession of parks, including

With connections to the regional transit system, this trail allows you to get to where you need to go.

Counties
Montgomery,
Prince George's

Endpoints
Baltimore Ave./US 1 and
Charles Armentrout Dr.
(Hyattsville) to Oakview
Dr. south of I-495 (Silver
Spring)

Mileage
7

Type
Greenway/Non-Rail-Trail

Roughness Index
1

Surface
Asphalt

Melrose Park, Magruder Park, and 38th Avenue Park. The route quickly crosses the waterway, rounds a bend, and then crosses the river once more. Shortly after the West Hyattsville Metro Station, the winding Sligo Creek Trail (see page 55) forks off to the northwest.

After crossing under East-West Highway/MD 410, the trail runs through dense woodlands that will make you forget you are in a major population center. The large Lane Manor Park next appears immediately to the east. At Adelphi Mill Park (near the trail's midpoint), visit the only surviving historic mill in Prince George's County, Adelphi Mill, built in 1796. Past the mill, the pathway reenters a wooded environment. A steep gravel connection at the trail's end climbs up to Oakview Drive, which leads to busy New Hampshire Avenue/MD 650.

If you are on foot or horse, you can choose to continue on the trail several miles farther north to Wheaton Regional Park—just don't take the gravel spur to Oakview Drive. This unpaved section is closed to bicyclists.

CONTACT: montgomeryparks.org/PPSD/ParkTrails/trails_MAPS
/NorthwestBranch.shtm

DIRECTIONS

Most of the parks along the trail's route have their own parking lots. Parking for the Northwest Branch Trail can be found at the southern endpoint at Anacostia River Park. From the Capital Beltway/I-495, take Exit 22. Head south for 3.6 miles on MD 295. Take the MD 450 exit toward Annapolis/Bladensburg (right), and continue on MD 450/Annapolis Road for 1.4 miles. Keep right to continue on Baltimore Ave./Alt. US 1 for 0.5 mile. The trail begins at the intersection of Baltimore Ave. and Charles Armentrout Dr.

Parking is also available at the trailhead just north of 40th Ave. From the Capital Beltway/I-495, take Exit 25. Travel south on US 1/Baltimore Ave. for 4.6 miles. Turn right onto Jefferson St. After 0.5 mile, turn left onto 40th Ave. Make a slight left at Hamilton St., and come to Magruder Park, where parking is available. Just ahead is a short path that connects to the trail.

At the trail's northern endpoint, you may park at Roscoe Nix Elementary School on Hedin Dr. in Silver Spring, MD. From the Capital Beltway/I-495, take Exit 28. Go south on MD 650/New Hampshire Ave. for 0.1 mile. Turn right onto Oakview Dr., and go 0.6 mile. Turn right onto Hedin Dr., and Roscoe Nix Elementary School will be to your immediate left.

13 Patuxent Branch Trail

The Patuxent Branch Trail is part of a 20-mile trail system over and around the rolling hills of Howard County. The route follows a former Baltimore & Ohio Railroad line along the Patuxent River.

The trail begins in Savage Park. Follow signs along the trail indicating the direction to Lake Elkhorn. When you reach Vollmerhausen Road, turn left. Stay on the sidewalk to find the trail where it picks up on the other side of the road at the bottom of this short hill. A crosswalk eases you across this busy road.

A little more than half of the route is paved (from Lake Elkhorn to the Pratt Bridge), and the other half has a gravel surface, which can get muddy in wet weather. A small portion of the trail includes a bridle path. Ten bridges help keep you dry as you travel through this

County
Howard

Endpoints
Savage Park (Savage) to
Lake Elkhorn (Columbia)

Mileage
4.6

Type
Rail-Trail

Roughness Index
1

Surface
Asphalt, Concrete,
Crushed Stone

Whatever the season, a trip along the Patuxent Branch Trail is a worthwhile excursion.

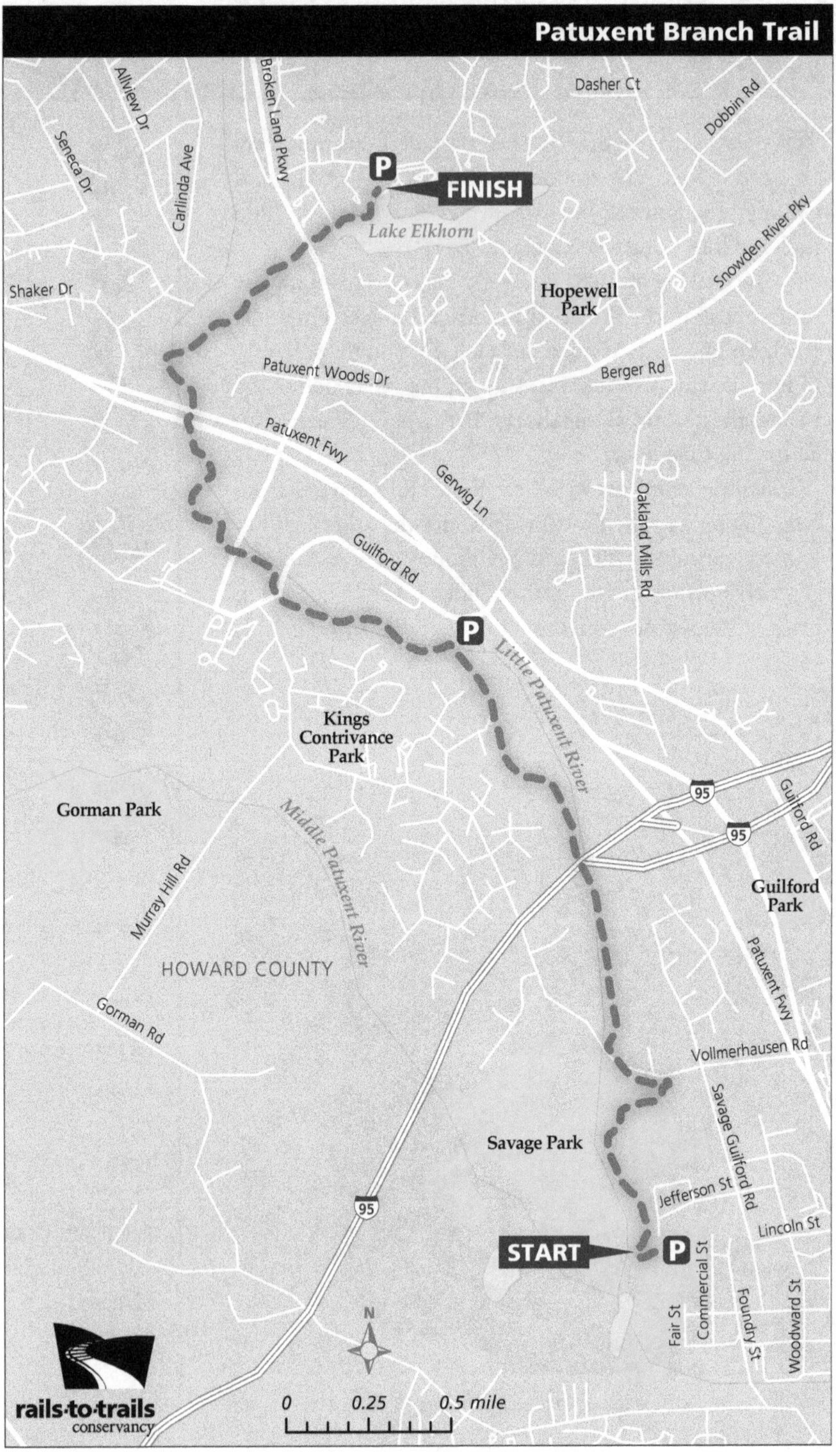

Patuxent Branch Trail

Dasher Ct

Allview Dr

Broken Land Pkwy

Dobbin Rd

Seneca Dr

Carlinda Ave

P

FINISH

Snowden River Pky

Lake Elkhorn

Shaker Dr

Hopewell Park

Patuxent Woods Dr

Berger Rd

Patuxent Fwy

Gerwig Ln

Oakland Mills Rd

Guilford Rd

P

Little Patuxent River

Kings Contrivance Park

Gorman Park

Middle Patuxent River

95

95

Guilford Rd

Murray Hill Rd

Guilford Park

HOWARD COUNTY

Patuxent Fwy

Gorman Rd

Vollmerhausen Rd

Savage Guilford Rd

Savage Park

95

Jefferson St

Lincoln St

START   **P**

Commercial St

Woodward St

Fair St

Foundry St

N

0   0.25   0.5 mile

rails·to·trails
conservancy

floodplain. The most impressive, the 1902 Guilford Pratt Truss Bridge, is a symbol of Howard County's two most important industries: the railroad and the granite quarry. Signs along the trail explain the historical significance of both industries, and the route will take you straight through the grounds of a quarry that operated until 1928.

The rail-trail ends at Lake Elkhorn, but picnic facilities, a playground, parking, a boat slip, and a walking and biking path around the lake may keep you going. Or you can head back to the Savage Park entrance of the Patuxent Branch Trail and pick up the flatter and shorter Savage Mill Trail (see page 53) that begins just a few blocks away on Foundry Street, near the entrance to the Historic Savage Mill.

CONTACT: **howardcountymd.gov/patuxentbranchtrail.htm**

DIRECTIONS

To access the Savage Park entrance from I-95, take Exit 38. Follow MD 32/Patuxent Fwy. east 1.1 miles to Exit 12. Turn right onto US 1/Baltimore Washington Blvd., heading south toward Laurel. After 0.5 mile, turn right onto Gorman Road, and then, after 0.4 mile, turn left onto Baltimore St. Follow it 0.6 mile to the end, where you take a right onto Fair St., which ends at the park. Take the road in the parking lot to the right until it ends at a smaller parking lot at the trailhead.

To access the Lake Elkhorn entrance from I-95, take Exit 38, and merge onto MD 32/Patuxent Fwy., heading west. After 1.9 miles, take Exit 14 to Broken Land Pkwy. and head north (right). The lake (and a parking lot next to the playground and boat slip) will be on your right.

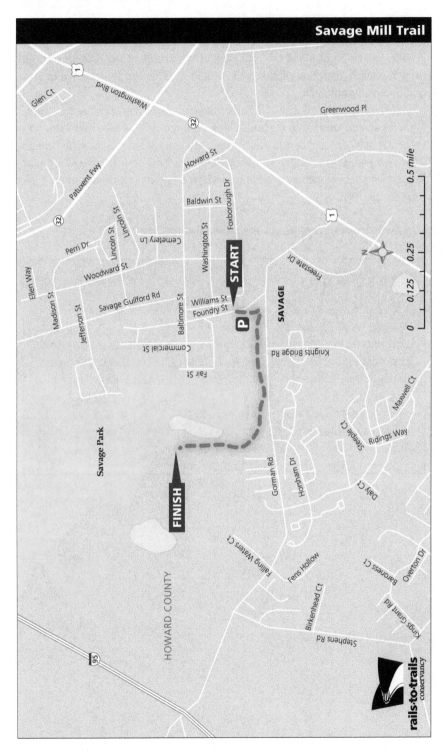

Savage Mill Trail

The Savage Mill Trail in Savage Park travels along the Patuxent River through the grounds of an old cotton mill. In the early 1800s, Savage was a major manufacturing center, harnessing power produced by the falls on the Little and Middle Patuxent Rivers. Near the trailhead stands an 1822 textile mill, today renovated as a shopping center where you can buy antiques or grab a picnic lunch to enjoy on the pleasant 0.8-mile trail.

The route begins at an old Bollman truss bridge, an iron structure used exclusively by the Baltimore and Ohio Railroad. Built in 1869, the bridge was moved to Savage in 1887. Though the company built about 100 of these bridges before 1873, only two of Wendel Bollman's bridges

County
Howard

Endpoints
Foundry St. to Savage Park (Savage)

Mileage
0.8

Type
Rail-Trail

Roughness Index
1

Surface
Asphalt, Dirt, Gravel

Though you are very near roads and a shopping center, the music of the river and the rustle of white oaks transport you away.

still exist in the States. The train tracks have been left in place on one side of the bridge, so you can imagine the train passing beside you as you ride or walk over this piece of history.

Most of the trail is paved and flat, but the surface changes to gravel and then dirt before it ends abruptly in the middle of the woods. Though you are near a major highway and the bustle of the shopping center, the music of the river rolling over large boulders and the white oaks enveloping the path create the impression that you're in the wilderness.

It's easy to stop and savor the natural oasis at one of the many picnic tables. The Savage Mill Trail is part of a larger, 20-mile system of pathways through Howard County. For a more challenging trip, hit the Patuxent Branch Trail (see page 49), which begins a few blocks away.

CONTACT: howardcountymd.gov

DIRECTIONS

From I-95, take Exit 38. Follow MD 32/Patuxent Fwy. east for 1.1 miles to Exit 12. Merge onto US 1/Baltimore Washington Blvd., heading south. After 0.5 mile, turn right onto Gorman Road and then, after 0.4 mile, right onto Foundry St. The Savage Mill parking lot is on your left.

15 Sligo Creek Trail

The Sligo Creek Trail parallels the eponymous waterway from its confluence with the Northwest Branch in Hyattsville to just north of its origin in Wheaton in Montgomery County. Along the way, a number of footbridges cross back and forth over the creek, and picnic areas and playgrounds line the route.

Part of the Anacostia Tributary Trail System, the trail is often referred to as one of the most scenic in the area. You're welcome to reach your own conclusion through comparison—Sligo Creek Trail connects to many other trails within the system. Begin your journey in Hyattsville, where the trail splits from the Northwest Branch

The Sligo Creek Trail offers a pleasant escape from the city as it sneaks in and out of the Maryland suburbs.

Counties
Montgomery,
Prince George's

Endpoints
West of Kirkwood Apartments at Nicholson St. and Ager Road (Hyattsville) to Wheaton Regional Park at Channing Dr. and Ventura Ave. (Wheaton)

Mileage
10.2

Type
Greenway/Non-Rail-Trail

Roughness Index
1

Surface
Asphalt

Sligo Creek Trail

Pine Lake Wheaton Regional Park

Arcola Ave

FINISH

Kemp Mill Estates Local Park

WHEATON

Georgia Ave

Breewood Park

University Blvd

Columbia Pike

29

WHITE OAK

MARYLAND

Paint Branch Park

MONTGOMERY COUNTY

Northwest Branch Park

29

P

P Argyle Park

Forest Glen Rd

495

495

HILLANDALE

495

Sligo Creek Park

Dale Dr

P

16th St

29

SILVER SPRING

Colesville Rd

Nolte Park

Long Branch–Wayne Local Park

Flower Ave

LANGLEY PARK

PRINCE GEORGE'S COUNTY

ADELPHI

University Blvd

Adelphi Park

P

Lane Manor Park

TAKOMA PARK

Rock Creek

Rock Creek Park

16th St NW

WASHINGTON, D.C.

Missouri Ave NW

13th St NW

Georgia Ave NW

29

CHILLUM

New Hampshire Ave NE

Fort Totten Park

Chillum Rd

S Dakota Ave NE

P

Green Meadows Park

Heurich Park

START

MT RAINIER

N

0 0.25 0.5   1 mile

rails·to·trails
conservancy

Trail (see page 47). Half a mile in, the path runs through Green Meadows Park, host to soccer fields, tennis courts, and other athletic facilities. While the trail occupies a central location in the urbanized Maryland suburbs of the District of Columbia, you would never know it while passing through the quiet and heavily wooded landscape.

A handful of neighborhood connector trails provides easy access for residents along the Sligo Creek Trail's route. After crossing busy New Hampshire Avenue/MD 650, the trail parallels Sligo Creek Parkway/MD 787. On a lovely day, you're likely to see more trail traffic than vehicular traffic on the road.

In Takoma Park, the route passes directly behind Washington Adventist Hospital and, farther north, past the property of Silver Spring's Holy Cross Hospital at I-495 (the Capital Beltway). After meandering a few more peaceful, tucked-away miles northward, the Sligo Creek Trail ends just south of the entrance to Wheaton Regional Park, a popular family destination, featuring a large playground, ice rink, fishing lake, picnic shelters, and even a merry-go-round and miniature train for the kids.

CONTACT: **montgomeryparks.org/PPSD/ParkTrails/trails_MAPS/sligo.shtm**

DIRECTIONS

Parking for the Sligo Creek Trail can be found in Chillum at Green Meadows Park. From I-495, take Exit 28B. Turn right onto MD 650/New Hampshire Ave. and continue for 2 miles. Turn left onto University Blvd. After 0.6 mile, turn right onto Riggs Road. After 0.8 mile, turn left onto MD 410/East-West Hwy. and take an immediate right onto 19th Pl., which soon merges with Sligo Pkwy. Green Meadows Park is 0.4 mile ahead on the left.

Farther north, parking is available at the intersection of Sligo Creek Pkwy. and Houston Ave. in Takoma Park. From I-495, take Exit 28B. Turn right onto MD 650/New Hampshire Ave. and continue for 1.1 miles. Turn right onto Piney Branch Road. After 1.2 miles, turn left onto Flower Ave. After 0.5 mile, turn right onto Houston Ave. Houston Ave. meets Sligo Creek Pkwy. in less than 0.5 mile.

Parking is also available just north of the intersection of Sligo Creek Pkwy. and Three Oaks Dr. in Silver Spring. From I-495, take Exit 29. Take US 29 south for 0.6 mile, and turn left onto Sligo Creek Pkwy. At 0.4 mile, the parkway intersects with Three Oaks Dr.

In Kemp Mill, park at the dedicated lot off Sligo Creek Pkwy. north of Dennis Ave. From I-495, take Exit 30. Turn right onto MD 193/University Blvd. and continue for 1.1 miles. Turn left onto Dennis Ave., which intersects with Sligo Creek Pkwy. in 0.6 mile.

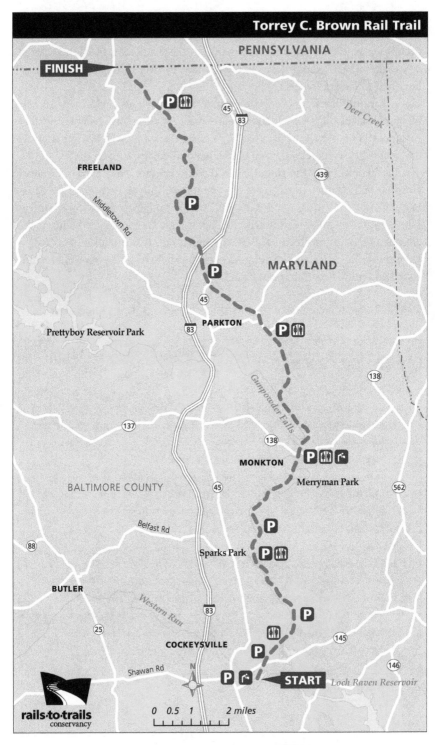

16 Torrey C. Brown Rail Trail

The Torrey C. Brown Rail Trail, completed in 1984, is one of the best hiking and biking trails in the Mid-Atlantic region. It allows for more than 20 miles of flat travel on the crushed-stone surface, punctuated by a number of access points and an abundance of trees that provide refreshing shade on hot summer days.

The trail begins in Cockeysville, Maryland, a suburb of Baltimore, and ends just over the state line in New Freedom, Pennsylvania, where the Mason-Dixon Line divides the southern Atlantic states from the Northeastern states. The history of the rail-trail dates back to 1832, when the Northern Central Railroad carried passengers—people vacationing at Bentley Springs—and freight between Baltimore and York or Harrisburg, Pennsylvania. The railroad

The trail provides a scenic natural escape from nearby city life.

County
Baltimore

Endpoints
Ashland Road (Cockeysville, MD) to MD–PA state line (New Freedom, PA)

Mileage
21

Type
Rail-Trail

Roughness Index
1

Surface
Crushed Stone

ran for about 140 years, and you can still see part of the old bed, which was converted to a rail-trail in the early 1980s.

Today, the Maryland Department of Natural Resources manages the Torrey C. Brown Trail as part of Gunpowder Falls State Park. Amenities along the route include picnic and park benches; drinking fountains for hikers, bikers, and four-legged friends; and portable restrooms. Just off the trail, you can enjoy a small art gallery, an antiques shop, and several places to buy food and drinks. Hotels and motels can be found within a mile of the trail, and a nearby bike shop rents and repairs bikes. The trail cuts through several charming Maryland towns: Monkton (a major stop for hikers and bikers), Parkton, Falls Overlook, and Bentley Springs. At the Maryland–Pennsylvania border near New Freedom, Pennsylvania, the trail continues as the Heritage Rail Trail County Park.

The trail is used by an eclectic mix of horseback riders, joggers, walkers, hikers, and bikers of all ages. On the weekends, local residents and travelers from the Baltimore area flock to the trail, so parking may be a challenge. For those seeking an escape from the urban areas of the region, this trail is a wooded oasis—an escape from the everyday stresses of nearby city life.

CONTACT: www.dnr.state.md.us/greenways/ncrt_trail.html

DIRECTIONS

To reach the MD 145/Ashland Road trailhead in Cockeysville, MD, from I-83, take Exit 20A toward Cockeysville. Merge onto Shawan Road. After 0.9 mile, turn right onto York Road. Take York for 0.3 mile, and turn left onto MD 145/Ashland Road. After 0.4 mile, turn right to stay on Ashland Road, and go another 0.2 mile to the trailhead.

To reach the trailhead at the MD–PA border (New Freedom, PA), from I-83, take Exit 4 toward Shrewsbury, and then turn east onto PA 851/E. Forrest Ave. After 0.7 mile, turn left onto S. Main St. Go 1.1 miles, and turn right onto Constitution Ave. After 1.9 miles, turn left onto E. High St., and go 0.3 mile. Turn right onto Singer Road. Take Singer Road 0.4 mile, and then take the third left (0.4 mile) onto Orwig Road. The trailhead is 0.5 mile ahead on your right.

There are numerous access points and parking areas along the route. Refer to the map for more details.

The first thing you may notice about Trolley Line #9 Trail is the boardwalk that curves between the bluffs of massive rock. The granite was hand cut in the 1890s when the electric streetcar rails were laid from Ellicott City to Catonsville. Today, these 100-foot-high walls create a striking gateway to the trail from historic Ellicott City just across the Patapsco River from Oella.

The boardwalk quickly turns to pavement as the route winds uphill through the woods. On your left, a babbling stream feeding into the Patapsco River provides a peaceful sound track to your journey. Tall shade trees keep the trail—and you—cool when you climb through the woodlands and occasionally pass homes that border the path. Near the 1-mile mark, a short detour off the trail will take you to Banneker Historical Park & Museum, which

Counties
Baltimore, Howard

Endpoints
Edmondson Ave. at Stonewall Road (Catonsville) to Oella Ave. (Ellicott City)

Mileage
1.5

Type
Rail-Trail

Roughness Index
1

Surface
Asphalt, Boardwalk

Rustic scenery and historical landmarks can be found along this short trail.

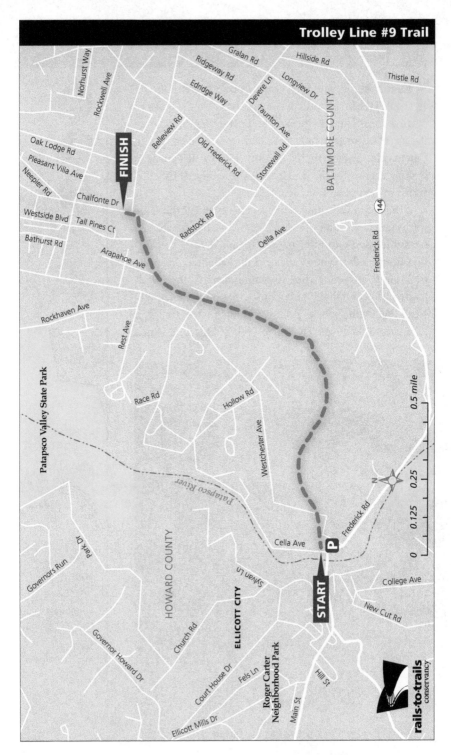

has nature trails, archaeological sites, and living history areas re-creating the Colonial farm life of Benjamin Banneker, an African American astronomer and farmer.

Back on the trail, the rustic scenery gives way to a more suburban landscape. The few road crossings are well marked, and the gradual slope makes for a pleasant trip both uphill and downhill. When you reach the end of the trail, simply turn around and head back downhill to enjoy Ellicott City, including the Baltimore & Ohio Train Museum, which highlights the history of the nation's first railroad.

CONTACT: **catonsvillerailstotrails.com/9-trolley-trail**

DIRECTIONS

To get to Ellicott City, take US 40 W from Baltimore, or take Exit 13, 14, or 15 from I-695. To get to Oella Ave. from downtown Ellicott City, take MD 144/Main St. east to the Patapsco River, where the street becomes Frederick Road. Cross the river and take an immediate left (north) onto Oella Ave., where you will find trail parking immediately on your right (the river is on your left). You must climb stairs to get to the trail from here.

For accessible parking, follow MD 144/Frederick Road east just past the Patapsco River and turn north (left) onto Westchester Ave. A small parking lot will be on your left, just before a switchback in the road.

To access the trail in Catonsville, from Baltimore, take I-95 South. Take Exit 49B for I-695. Take I-695 north for 2.7 miles to Exit 14. Turn left onto Edmondson Ave. At 2.6 miles, Edmondson meets Stonewall Road. This is where the trail ends.

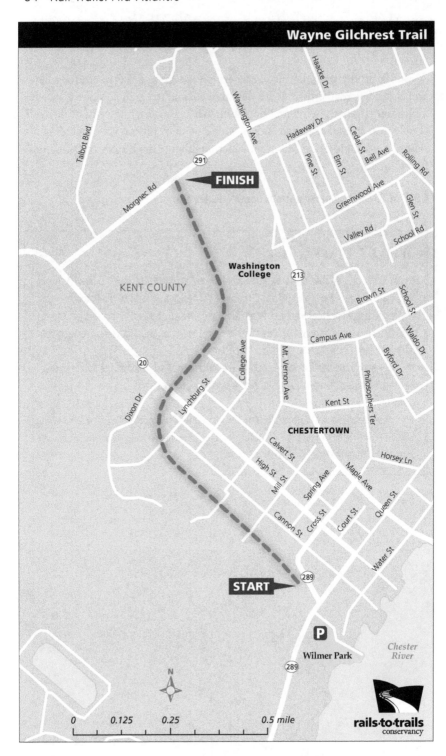

The Wayne Gilchrest Trail, which opened on Earth Day in 2012, runs along the southern edge of the historic Maryland Eastern Shore community of Chestertown. The trail connects Washington College to the Chestertown business district.

Start your journey at popular Wilmer Park on the Chester River. The trail begins just across South Cross Street/MD 289 from the park, where an original train station has been converted to office use. Because the Wayne Gilchrest Trail occupies a former rail corridor that last saw freight service in the early 1990s, trail users are treated to a flat surface and gentle curves.

From the old train station, the rail-trail parallels Cannon Street adjacent to some of the town's charming residences. A turn to the northeast shortly thereafter takes

County
Kent

Endpoints
S. Cross St./MD 289 and S. Queen St. to Morgnec Road/MD 291 at Washington College (Chestertown)

Mileage
1.2

Type
Rail-Trail

Roughness Index
1

Surface
Asphalt

The Wayne Gilchrest Trail runs along the southern edge of the historic community of Chestertown.

bikers and walkers to High Street. In the future, Chestertown plans to construct an extension to the trail bordering High Street; this spur will connect to additional residences to the north of the town.

Across High Street, the route passes an industrial property before entering the campus of Washington College. The path proceeds along the entire length of the campus of the 10th-oldest college in the country before ending at Morgnec Road/MD 291.

CONTACT: **chestertown.com**

DIRECTIONS

Parking for the Wayne Gilchrest Trail can be found at the southern trailhead at Wilmer Park. From the intersection of Chestertown Road, Morgnec Road, and High St. in Chestertown, travel approximately 1 mile on High St., and turn right onto S. Cross St. The park is on the left along the Chester River.

Alternatively, park on the campus of Washington College near the trail's northern endpoint at Morgnec Road/MD 291. The trailhead is 0.4 mile from the intersection of Chestertown Road, Morgnec Road, and High St. in Chestertown.

19 Western Maryland Rail Trail

Plan a full day (or two) for your visit to the Western Maryland Rail Trail, a 22-mile paved route that will take you through several eras of American history.

You can access this trail from many points, but the main trailhead is in the quaint town of Hancock (population 1,750). Stop here for food, drinks, or antiques shopping; stay the night or simply wander around the historical downtown, which was once Maryland's frontier and was frequently visited by George Washington, among other notables.

From the trailhead in Hancock, you can head east or west along the trail, about 10 miles in either direction. Whichever direction you choose, expect to pass fields and wooded groves. The rail-trail parallels the Chesapeake and Ohio Canal, a 185-mile, unpaved towpath that was used

County
Washington

Endpoints
Big Pool Road near Fort Frederick State Park to Old Pearre Rail Station (Sideling Hill WMA)

Mileage
22

Type
Rail-Trail

Roughness Index
1

Surface
Asphalt

A trip along the Western Maryland Rail Trail is an interactive history lesson.

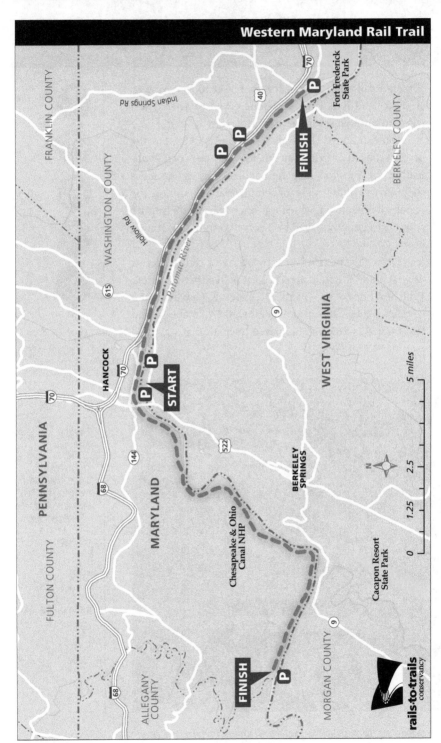

Western Maryland Rail Trail

to transport coal from Cumberland, Maryland, to the port of Georgetown in Washington, D.C., from 1828 until 1924. The route's historical sites include the canal's locks and lockhouses.

The western portion of the Western Maryland Rail Trail is blessed with magnificent views of the Potomac River. Large rock outcrops will catch your attention, as will the ruins of the Round Top Cement Mill, which was built in the 1830s and was Hancock's largest employer during the Civil War.

To the east, and just past downtown Hancock, you can buy trailside snacks from Blue Goose Fruit Market & Bakery, where, in the 1920s, more than 5,000 surrounding acres were planted with fruit trees. Traveling a little farther, you will find historical markers for Little Pool and Park Head Cemeteries. Be on the lookout for deer and wild turkey, which are not fazed by the loud traffic nearby (nor are the bears occasionally spotted in the area).

At trail's end, hop on the C&O Canal Towpath and continue just a short distance east to Fort Frederick, which is well worth a visit. To vary your route and maximize your scenery, take the Western Maryland Rail Trail in one direction and loop back on the towpath.

CONTACT: dnr2.maryland.gov/publiclands/Pages/western/wmrt.aspx

DIRECTIONS

Fort Frederick State Park trailhead: From I-70, take Exit 12 to MD 56 and head east toward Big Pool for 0.2 mile. The trail parking lot is across the street from the post office.

Hancock trailhead: From I-70, take Exit 3 and travel west (right) on MD 144 for 1.4 miles. Parking is at Hancock Station, just off Main St.

Sideling Hill Wildlife Management Area trailhead: From I-68, take Exit 77. Take a left (west) on MD 144, and then immediately take a right (south) on Woodmont Road. Continue for 6.4 miles on Woodmont, which will intersect with the trail at Pearre Road. Parking is available.

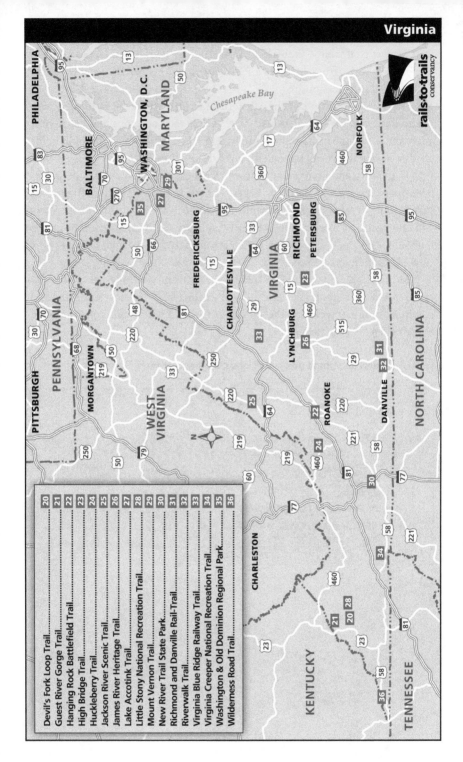

Virginia

rails-to-trails
conservancy

Virginia

A trestle along the New River Trail transports riders over the trail's namesake waterway.

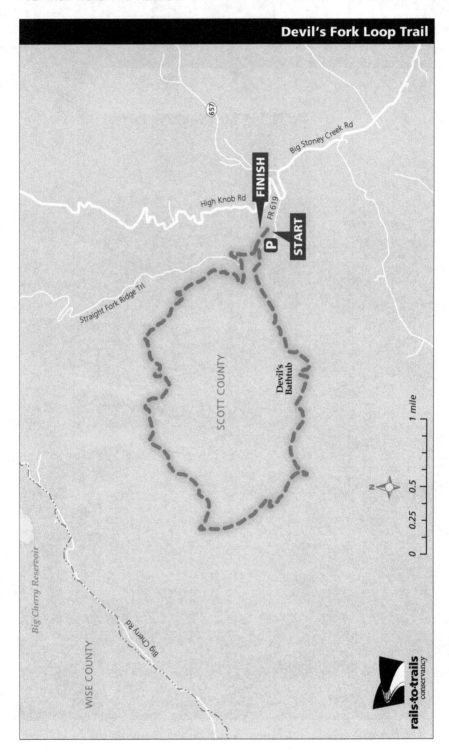

Devil's Fork Loop Trail

657

Big Stoney Creek Rd

FINISH

High Knob Rd

FR 619

P

START

Straight Fork Ridge Trl

SCOTT COUNTY

Devil's Bathtub

Big Cherry Reservoir

Big Cherry Rd

WISE COUNTY

N

0   0.25   0.5   1 mile

rails-to-trails
conservancy

The Devil's Fork Loop Trail provides an impressively beautiful route through an old-growth hemlock and rhododendron forest. The trail is extremely challenging, with as many as 18 stream crossings (at the height of the winter thaw), a 1,200-foot elevation change, and many opportunities to lose the path. Be sure to bring enough water for this strenuous hike; there are no facilities on or near the trail. Amazing rock formations, waterfalls, swimming holes, and mountain views give you plenty to see and do, but keep one eye on the trail, as the going can be rough. Though the route follows yellow blazes for its entire 7 miles, poor maintenance means that it is often difficult to find the blazes and the path, which, in several places, scrambles over large rocks or up very steep cliff faces.

For gorgeous waterfalls and emerald pools, take a hike on the Devil's Fork Loop Trail.

County
Scott

Endpoints
Forest Road 619 (Jefferson National Forest, near Fort Blackmore, VA)

Mileage
7

Type
Rail-Trail

Roughness Index
3

Surface
Dirt

The western leg of the loop follows the Devil's Fork, and your first crossing is about 0.25 mile from the parking lot. Be prepared to get your feet wet. This, like many of the trail's water crossings, has very slippery rocks and seasonally changing water levels. After this, the trail breaks in two directions. The less strenuous route is to the left, following the loop clockwise. This also lets you hit the highlights of the trail much earlier.

The only hint that you are on a rail-trail is the abandoned coal car that sits about halfway up Little Mountain. In fact, the western side of the loop is the only portion on an old railbed. This railroad was used to transport logs and coal, and thus the corridor is not as wide as a standard-gage railway, and the grade is much steeper, which provided the trains with better access to these resources.

The trail's main attraction is Devil's Bathtub, located just 1.5 miles from the start. The rushing water of Devil's Fork shoots out of the soft sandstone and swirls quickly through this stone slide, plummeting into a beautiful pool of blue-green water. Another highlight, shortly after Devil's Bathtub, is the 50-foot waterfall at the mouth of Corder Hollow. The trail enters a very different landscape as you leave the Devil's Fork and begin hiking along the ridges of several mountains. The forest has little underbrush, and the path can be easily lost.

Your adventure concludes on an old logging road with about a mile of steep switchbacks to the loop's end, where you cross Devil's Fork for the last time. Primitive camping facilities are near the parking lot. You can continue hiking by taking the Straight Fork Ridge Trail (1.8 miles) via the parking lot. The scenery on Straight Fork Ridge is similar to the Devil's Fork Loop Trail, but the latter is considered the more interesting of the two.

CONTACT: www.fs.usda.gov/gwj

DIRECTIONS

From Alt. US 58 in Coeburn, take VA 72 south toward Fort Blackmore for 11.5 miles. In Dungannon, VA 72 merges with VA 65. Just before they separate in Fort Blackmore, at another 8.2 miles, take VA 619/Big Stoney Creek Road/High Knob Road to the right. Continue on VA 619 for 4.4 miles (taking a right and then a left to stay on VA 619); look for the Devil's Fork sign where VA 619 takes a sharp left and becomes Forest Road 619 (there is no street sign). Travel over the one-lane bridge and turn left just before the abandoned white house. Follow this unmarked dirt road to the end, where you will find parking for the trail. The road to the parking lot is very rutted and may not be accessible by all vehicles. You will pass the trailhead on your right just before you reach the parking lot; stairs lead up to the trail from the parking lot.

Alternatively, you can take US 23/58/421 (Daniel Boone Heritage Hwy.) toward Gate City. In Gate City, go straight on Bus. US 23/58/421 as the road becomes E. Jackson St. and, ultimately, VA 71. Head east on VA 71 for a little more than a mile. From here, take VA 72/Veterans Memorial Hwy. to the left for 10.9 miles to Fort Blackmore. Shortly after VA 65 and VA 72 merge, turn left onto VA 619/Big Stoney Creek Road/High Knob Road. From here, follow the directions above.

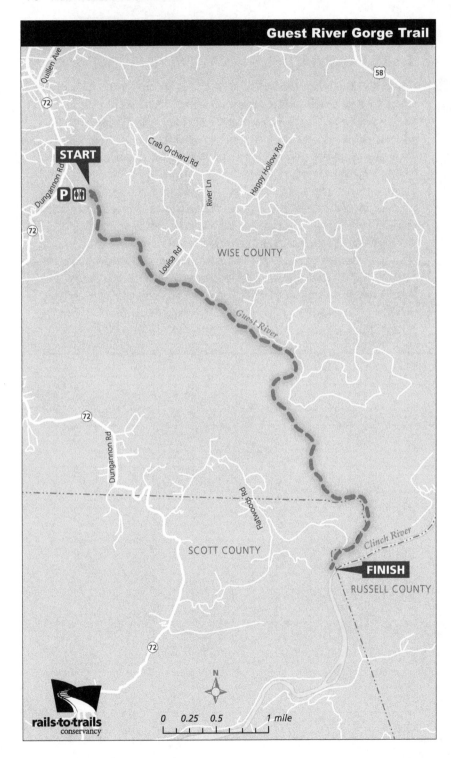

Guest River Gorge Trail

21 Guest River Gorge Trail

The Guest River Gorge Trail meanders beside 300-million-year-old sandstone cliffs that plunge 400 feet to the pristine waters below. The Guest River, now designated as a state scenic river, tunneled through Stone Mountain on its way toward the Clinch River, creating the deep gorge.

The gentle grade of this trail and its gravel surface make it ideal for a comfortable walk or bike ride. Benches along the route offer more than a place to rest; they yield stunning views of crystal-clear currents that, when interrupted sporadically by boulders, turn into impressive rapids.

In addition to spectacular Guest River views to the south, the trail offers a trip through the Swede Tunnel, built in 1922. The path also crosses three bridges over

This trail skirts the edge of the vast Jefferson National Forest.

Counties
Scott, Wise

Endpoints
VA 755 near river to
Forest Road 2477 (Jefferson National Forest)

Mileage
5.8

Type
Rail-Trail

Roughness Index
2

Surface
Crushed Stone

small creeks that replaced the trestles once traveled by rail cars, which hauled coal mined nearby.

Be sure to look for devil's walkingstick, a plant native to the Southeast and a member of the ginseng family. This tall and spindly plant produces white blooms during July and August.

Near the end, the trail slopes downhill toward a working rail line across the Guest River. Just before this point, you will see a connection to the Heart of Appalachia Bike Route, which stretches another 125 miles to Burke's Garden in Tazewell County, Virginia. Legend has it that Burke's Garden is so beautiful that it was originally sought after as the location for George Washington Vanderbilt's Biltmore Estate. However, the people of Burke's Garden refused to sell him any land, and thus he built his estate in Asheville, North Carolina, instead.

CONTACT: www.fs.usda.gov/gwj

DIRECTIONS

The Guest River Gorge Trail is an out-and-back, so there is only one endpoint. From Alt. US 58 in Coeburn, head south on VA 72. Travel for 2.3 miles on this curvy, two-lane road. You will pass the Flatwoods Picnic Area on your right; very soon afterward, you will reach a sign for the Guest River Gorge on your left. Turn left onto this paved road, which is Forest Road 2477, and drive for 1.4 miles until you reach the parking lot. The trailhead is marked with a kiosk at the edge of the parking area.

22 Hanging Rock Battlefield Trail

Opened in 1999, the Hanging Rock Battlefield Trail in Salem (just outside of Roanoke) is associated with southern Virginia's impressive Civil War history. The northern trailhead at Hanging Rock was the site of the 1864 Hunter's Raid, in which General John McCausland's Confederate forces won a substantial victory against the retreating Union Army under the command of General David Hunter. A monument marks the site along VA 311.

Start at the Hanging Rock trailhead, but understand that this is primarily a pleasant walk if you're already in the neighborhood, not necessarily a destination trail. Parking is plentiful, and you can hit the convenience store and gas station next door to stock up on provisions. On the trail, you can absorb the Roanoke Valley's beautiful wooded scenery; the corridor winds along Mason Creek

History buffs will love the Hanging Rock Battlefield Trail.

County
Roanoke

Endpoints
Kessler Mill Road near Branch Dr. to VA 311 (Salem)

Mileage
1.7

Type
Rail-Trail

Roughness Index
1

Surface
Asphalt, Concrete

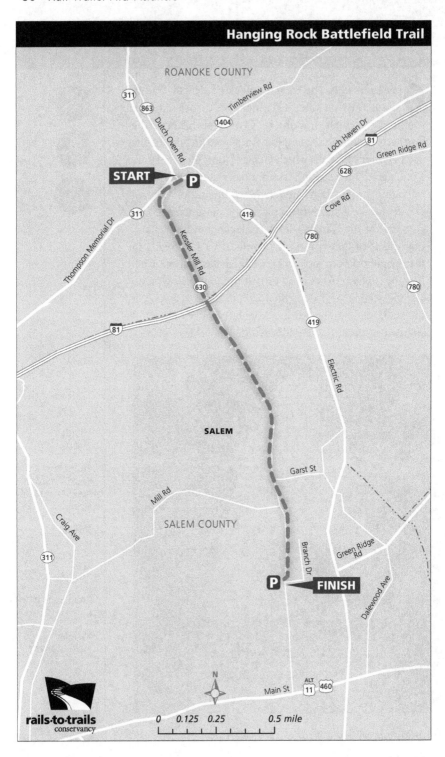

and Kessler Mill Road. After passing under I-81, you will soon enter the township of Salem. The trail curves through a residential area, and houses flank the path until you reach the southern trailhead at Timberview Road. If time permits, on your return to the northern trailhead, take a quick jaunt on the short hiking trail at the Hanging Rock trailhead. It meanders along Peter's Creek right up to I-81.

CONTACT: **roanokecountyparks.com/Facilities/Facility/Details**
/Hanging-Rock-Battlefield-Trail-17

DIRECTIONS

To reach the Hanging Rock trailhead from I-81, take Exit 141 (VA 419 toward Salem/New Castle). Turn north onto VA 419 and continue on VA 311 for 0.4 mile. The parking area for the Hanging Rock Battlefield Trail is on the left (adjacent to the parking area for the convenience store) or across VA 311 at the monument.

To reach the southern terminus from I-81, take Exit 141 (VA 419 toward Salem/New Castle). Turn south on VA 419/N. Electric Road. Go approximately 1 mile and turn right onto Dalewood Ave. Take the first left onto Garst St. Turn left onto Kessler Mill Road, and drive 0.5 mile to the parking lot on the right.

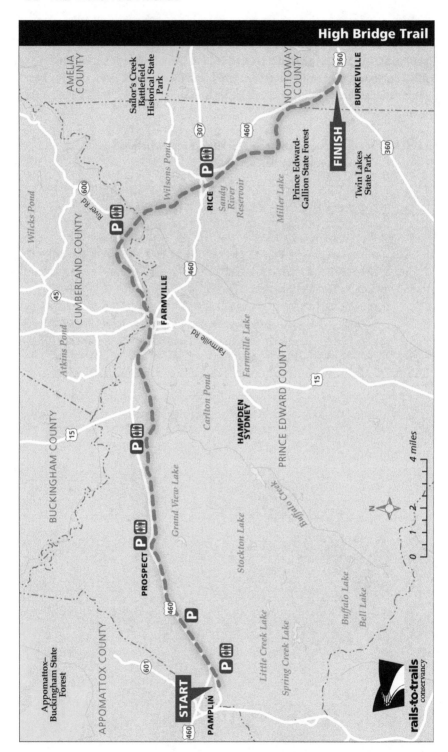

23 High Bridge Trail

The central feature for which the High Bridge Trail is named towers 107 feet above the mighty Appomattox River and stretches nearly 0.5 mile (2,418 feet) across it. The bridge's breathtaking view of the surrounding Central Virginia countryside, combined with the ease of getting here (the trail is only about an hour's drive from both Lynchburg and Richmond), makes it a must-see destination.

During the Civil War, the bridge—now included on the National Register of Historic Places—was a strategic point for both Union and Confederate soldiers; both armies made attempts to destroy it to prevent the other side from crossing the river. About a dozen miles from the west end of the High Bridge Trail lies the famed Appomattox Court House, where General Robert E. Lee finally surrendered. Several museums and other historical attractions in Appomattox make the town a worthwhile side trip.

This trail's centerpiece, High Bridge, played a role in a battle near the end of the Civil War.

Counties
Cumberland, Nottoway, Prince Edward

Endpoints
CR 660 (Pamplin) to US 460 (near Burkeville)

Mileage
32.4

Type
Rail-Trail

Roughness Index
1

Surface
Crushed Stone

Those looking for a short, easy outing can begin their journey in the charming town of Farmville. From downtown, riders and hikers will have only 4.5 miles to go to reach the bridge, following the wide, gentle grade of the former South Side Railroad, a spur off the Norfolk Southern Railway. Along the way, look for the railroad's mile-marker posts dating back to the 1850s; those marked with "N" list the distance from Norfolk, while those labeled with a "W" notified railroad engineers to blow their whistles. (For an even shorter excursion, a closer parking lot is available at River Road, about a mile from the bridge.)

For the more adventurous, the rail-trail extends outward from west to east from the trailhead in Pamplin, totaling more than 30 miles through woodlands and rural farmland. The trail's surface of finely crushed limestone is well suited for hybrid and mountain bikes, and horseback riding is also permitted. Restrooms are available en route, but drinking water is not, so be sure to pack some.

In addition to Farmville, the communities of Pamplin, Prospect, and Rice are connected by the trail. The trail's eastern end lies just outside of Burkeville.

CONTACT: dcr.virginia.gov/state-parks/high-bridge-trail.shtml

DIRECTIONS

To access the trail from the western trailhead in Pamplin, from Lynchburg, follow US 460 E a little more than 25 miles, and turn right onto Bus. US 460 E/Pamplin Road. After 2 miles, turn right onto CR 660, and make an immediate left to the trailhead.

To reach the eastern trailhead in Burkeville, from Richmond, take US 360 W for approximately 40 miles. In Burkeville, about 2 miles after US 360 merges with US 460, turn left onto VA 621. After 0.5 mile on VA 621, make a sharp left onto VA T-716 (which immediately becomes VA 716). The trail is on the left.

Parking (a fee is required) is also available at the following locations (west to east):

In Elam: Immediately off US 460 at Sulpher Spring Road, near trail milepost 164

In Prospect (wheelchair accessible; designated horse trailer parking): On Prospect Road just off US 460, near trail milepost 161

In Tuggle: On Tuggle Road, 0.7 mile off US 460, near trail milepost 156

In Farmville (designated horse trailer parking): Take US 15 N to Bus. US 15 N, and continue for about 2.5 miles. Look for the municipal lots where the trail intersects Main St., near milepost 150. To reach the River Road lot from here, continue on N. Main St. for 0.4 mile, and turn right onto River Road. After 3.1 miles, the parking lot for the trail will be on your left.

In Rice (wheelchair accessible): On Depot Road, 0.25 mile off US 460, near trail milepost 142

In the early 1900s, a train line nicknamed the Huckleberry was built to transport coal and provide mail and passenger service to Blacksburg. The line was also used by the Corps of Cadets at Virginia Polytechnic Institute (more commonly known as Virginia Tech), who unofficially renamed Blacksburg "Huckleberry Junction" because of the abundance of huckleberries that grew along the train line. The berries began growing after trees were cleared for railroad construction; thereafter, the region became famous for delicious pies and jams. Though the amount of huckleberries along the route today has diminished, trail users can find huckleberry bushes planted around information kiosks.

The Huckleberry Trail is a mix of rural and rolling landscape—sometimes forested, sometimes wide open—and town life, as the route starts and ends in city centers.

A bend in the tracks along Huckleberry Trail

County
Montgomery

Endpoints
Draper Road
(Blacksburg) to the
Christiansburg Recreation Center at Cambria
St. (Christiansburg)

Mileage
7.9

Type
Rail-Trail

Roughness Index
1

Surface
Asphalt

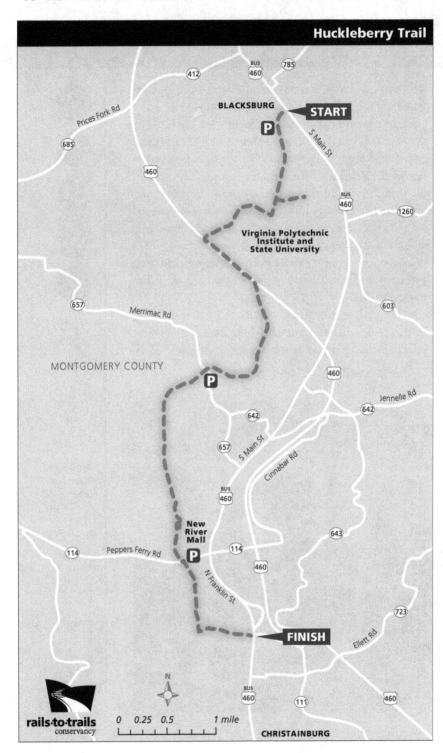

The northern trailhead is nestled in a residential neighborhood at the Blacksburg Branch Library in downtown Blacksburg, across from the Virginia Tech campus. You may hear a marching band in the distance or notice a game at the nearby Worsham Field on campus. As you continue along this meandering path, you leave the city and enter a rural setting, passing behind quiet homes and through open fields and pockets of forests. Crossing under US 460, take care to stay with the Huckleberry as it heads southeast along the highway. Other options lead you to the roadway or fade away into farm fields.

The Coal Mining Heritage Park at mile 4, just before you reach a railroad bridge over the still-active Norfolk Southern rail line, displays old mining equipment. Unlike most rail-trails, this one has many gentle curves and slopes, providing diversity in your experience. In fact, on these steeper sections, the old trains reportedly slowed down enough for cadets to hop from the cars and pick huckleberries before the train gathered more speed.

The trailhead north of New River Valley Mall in Christiansburg is the former terminus of the trail. Now you can either plow up the steep hillside to the mall-side pocket park (one of many on the trail), or branch off to the west around the base of the hill to run adjacent to the active rail line. A new bridge over VA 114 continues the trail behind big-box stores to Cambria Street and the trail's current endpoint at the Christiansburg Recreation Center.

CONTACT: huckleberrytrail.org

DIRECTIONS

To reach the northern trailhead, take US 460 toward Blacksburg and take Exit 5. Turn onto Main St. (take the Bus. US 460 route), heading north. After 2.9 miles, turn left onto Miller St., heading southwest, and drive three blocks to Harrell St., where street parking is available. The trailhead is located in the library parking lot on Miller St. However, avoid using this lot; towing may be enforced for trail users parked here.

To reach parking near New River Valley Mall, take US 460 toward Christiansburg, and take Exit 4. Turn right onto VA 114/Peppers Ferry Road. The New River Valley Mall is on the right on New River Road, less than 0.5 mile from the exit. Follow New River Road, which loops around the mall; trailhead parking is at the back of the mall.

To reach the trail's southern terminus, take US 460 and exit toward Bus. US 460 E/Downtown. Continue onto N. Franklin St. for 0.2 mile, and turn right onto Cambria St. NW. The Christiansburg Recreation Center and parking lot are to the right.

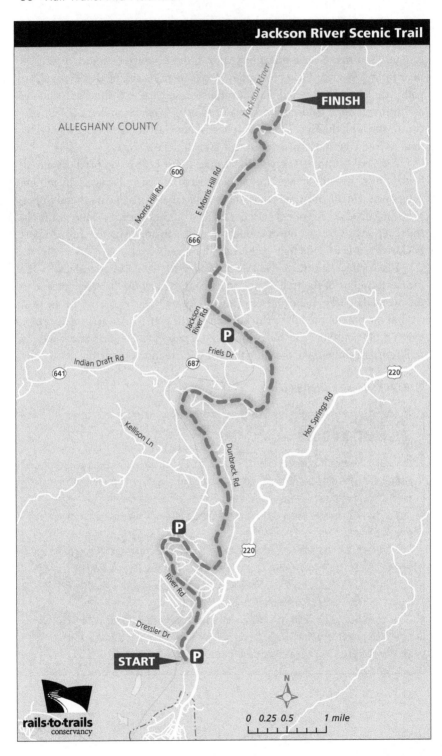

25 Jackson River Scenic Trail

Waterfalls, river views, rugged rock formations, vibrant fall foliage, and delicate flowers in the spring: These are the sights that put the *scenic* in Jackson River Scenic Trail. The peaceful rail-trail, nestled in the Allegheny Highlands of western Virginia, traces the route of what was once the Hot Springs Branch of the Chesapeake and Ohio Railway.

It begins in Intervale, just north of Covington, and winds north, hugging the curves of its namesake river. Picnic benches along the water allow you to rest and take in the beautiful surroundings. For added adventure, you can kayak or canoe in the river, and it's also known as an excellent place for trout fishing.

The trail's crushed gravel surface stops at the Smith Bridge trailhead; north from there, the trail has a natural,

Much of the Jackson River Scenic Trail runs through lush woodlands.

County
Alleghany

Endpoints
Dressler Dr., off US 220 (just north of Covington) to Jackson River Road at VA 637 (Hot Springs)

Mileage
10.7

Type
Rail-Trail

Roughness Index
2

Surface
Dirt, Grass, Gravel

grassy surface to its end at Hot Springs. Much of the route is wooded, and you may see deer, rabbits, groundhogs, and other wildlife.

Round out your experience with a visit to the C&O Depot in Covington for a peek at the trail's railroad past. The restored 1908 structure now houses the Alleghany Historical Society and its exhibits on the history of the region. Rail buffs may also want to head 11 miles east of Covington to Clifton Forge, where many historical railroad artifacts and equipment are on display at the C&O Railway Heritage Center.

Another nearby and worthwhile side trip is the Falling Spring Overlook. The roadside attraction is a jaw-dropping 80-foot waterfall on US 220, just north of Covington.

CONTACT: jacksonrivertrail.com

DIRECTIONS

Take I-64 to Exit 16A (Covington/Hot Springs). There are three parking areas for the trail:

Just north of Covington at US 220 and Dressler Dr. From the interstate exit, turn left onto US 220/US 60. Continue on US 220 for 4.1 miles, and turn left onto VA 778/Dressler Dr. The trailhead is immediately on your right.

In Clearwater Park on Jackson River Road across from Petticoat Junction. From the interstate exit, follow US 220 for 5.1 miles, and turn left onto VA 687/Jackson River Road. Follow it for 1 mile, and Petticoat Junction will be on your right, just before your cross over Jackson River.

At the Smith Bridge parking lot on VA 721, 0.5 mile off VA 687. From the interstate exit, follow US 220 for 5.1 miles, and turn left onto VA 687/Jackson River Road. Follow it for 4.7 miles. Turn right onto VA 721, and follow it 0.6 mile to Smith Bridge Road. The trail parking lot is on your right.

26 James River Heritage Trail (Blackwater Creek Natural Area)

The James River Heritage Trail in the Blackwater Creek Natural Area is one of the premier urban trails in the state, passing through lush forest as well as the heart of historic, industrial downtown Lynchburg. It offers multiple easy connections to other trails along the way, and the route is well marked with trail and mileage signs. Mountain bikes are permitted but should give way to foot traffic.

The 9.5-mile trail is actually an interconnected system of shorter trails, each with a different name: Blackwater Creek Bikeway, Kemper Station Trail, Point of Honor Trail, RiverWalk, and Percival's Island Trail.

The Blackwater Creek Bikeway begins at the Ed Page trailhead (with nice facilities) on Old Langhorne Road. Take a minute to stroll through the pleasant Awareness Garden, dedicated to persons with cancer. From here, the

The Hollins Tunnel is a highlight of the trail.

Counties
Amherst, Lynchburg

Endpoints
Old Langhorne Road to 0.5 mile east of Fertilizer Road (Lynchburg)

Mileage
9.5

Type
Rail-Trail

Roughness Index
1

Surface
Asphalt, Dirt, Wood Chips

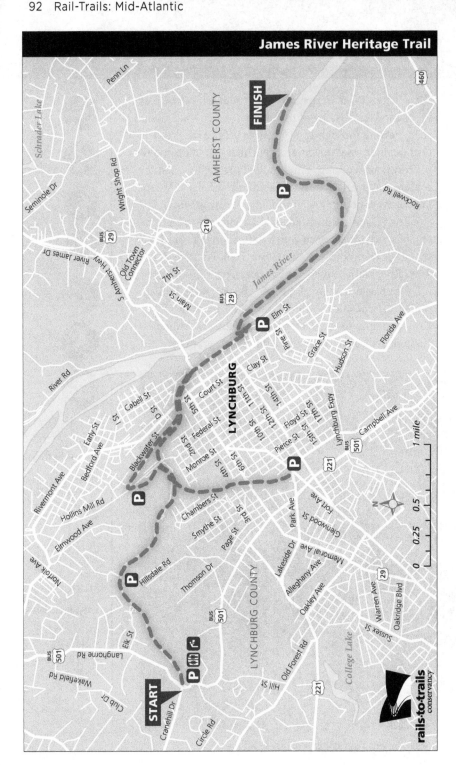

route follows an old railroad grade for 3 miles to Jefferson Street downtown, near where the creek flows into the James River. Along the way, the trail traverses the Blackwater Creek Natural Area, and a few unpaved paths lead into the woods down a steep bank to the creek. Shortly after you go under the railroad bridge, high above you near mile 2, the trail branches off to the left (north) and becomes the Point of Honor Trail (1.75 miles long). To the right (south), you'll find the Kemper Station Trail, 1 mile long to the Kemper Street Station. If you take the Kemper Station Trail, you'll have to backtrack to return to the main trail.

If you continue on the main Blackwater Creek Bikeway instead of taking the Point of Honor spur, you will go through the funky Hollins Tunnel, nearly 0.5 mile long. The tunnel bends but is well lit, and water seeps from the ceiling. If you take the Point of Honor Trail, you'll cross a spillway; use caution when water is flowing over the top. If the water is too high and fast, you can cross above the spillway at the road.

At mile 3 (3.75 if you take the Point of Honor Trail), the Blackwater Creek Bikeway meets up with the RiverWalk, a 1-mile segment along Jefferson Street's sidewalks to Washington Street. At Washington, turn left (north), cross the tracks, and continue on the trail, where it becomes Percival's Island Trail. You will cross a spectacular refurbished railroad bridge onto the island. Stop at the overlook for views back upriver toward downtown. The path traverses the 1-mile-long island before crossing a second former rail bridge to the eastern shore of the James River. Back on the mainland, private property surrounds the trail, and signs warn you to keep to the trail to avoid trespassing.

The James River Heritage Trail continues for another 1.25 miles along the river's edge until its end less than a mile past the last access point, off of Fertilizer Road. When you reach the endpoint, the railroad corridor clearly continues, but the trail becomes a dirt track that eventually crosses the river again after going under US 29, emerging onto VA 726/Mt. Athos Road.

CONTACT: **lynchburgva.gov/trails**

DIRECTIONS

To reach the Blackwater Creek Bikeway trailhead from the intersection of US 501 and Bus. US 501/Boonsboro Road, travel 2.9 miles on Bus. US 501. Turn right to continue on Bus. US 501/Langhorne Road. After 1.4 miles, turn left onto Old Langhorne Road. The trailhead will be on your left. From Lynchburg Expy./Bus. US 29, take Exit 3. Follow US 221 briefly to get on Bus. US 501, which becomes Langhorne Road, and go north for 3 miles. Be on the lookout for a quick right turn onto Old Langhorne Road; the trailhead is on the right.

To reach the Fertilizer Road trailhead from Lynchburg Expy./Bus. US 29, take the VA 210/Old Town Connector exit. Turn right onto VA 210 and then, after 0.2 mile, right again onto Colony Road. After 0.8 mile, take a slight left onto Carolina Ave. At 0.4 mile, take the second left onto Fertilizer Road, and turn right to follow it all the way (0.3 mile) to the trailhead for parking.

You can hop on the James River Heritage Trail from many other places along its route. Drop by the Lynchburg Visitor Information Center (216 12th St.; 800-732-5821) for detailed maps of the trail system.

In Northern Virginia's suburban community of Springfield, Lake Accotink Park provides a wilderness escape amid the city surroundings. The 500-acre park features picnic areas, miniature golf, an antique carousel, a 55-acre lake with canoe and kayak rentals, and, of course, trails. The Lake Accotink Trail follows part of the former railbed of the Orange and Alexandria Railroad, along which soldiers and materials were transported during the Civil War. Historical markers outline the railroad's history and help mark the entry to the park.

At the trail's start, it's impossible to miss the still-operating trestle bridge high above Accotink Creek. The creek's dam, constructed more than 50 years ago, created a popular fishing hole. As you leave the picnic and boat-rental area behind, the trail shoots up a short, steep hill

County
Fairfax

Endpoints
Marina at Lake Accotink
Park to Heming Ave.
(Springfield)

Mileage
4.5

Type
Rail-Trail

Roughness Index
2

Surface
Asphalt, Crushed Stone,
Gravel

Lake Accotink Trail is a popular destination for Northern Virginians looking for peace and quiet.

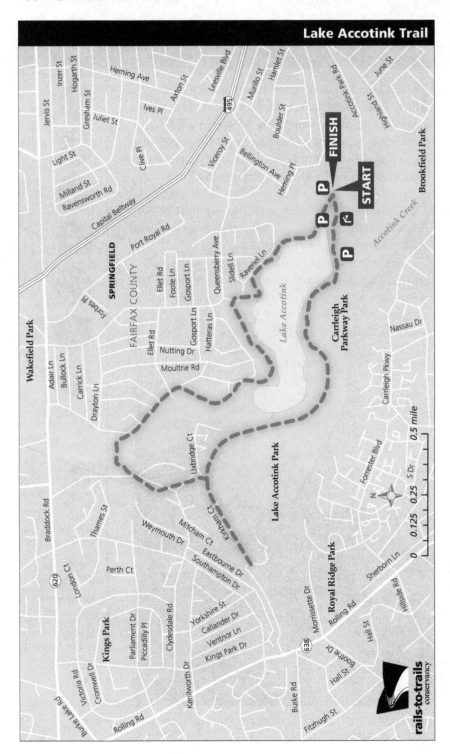

Lake Accotink Trail

toward the woods surrounding the lake. (If that seems daunting, do the route in reverse and take the 60-degree hill on its descent instead.) The first half of this route hugs the lake's curves as it travels deeper into the small woodlands preserve that provides shade and wonderful views of the marshland and lake.

When you reach the fork in the road at the trail's midpoint, you have two options. Continue straight for another 0.75-mile jaunt on the rail-trail before it dead-ends at Rolling Road, or follow the trail marker indicating a right turn to loop back to your starting point. This 4.5-mile option takes you down a short hill, onto neighborhood sidewalks for three or four blocks, and past an elementary school before you return to the park. On the main route, several stairs lead downhill to a bridge and back to the Lake Accotink Trail, which circles around the other side of the lake, to the creek and surrounding marshland. Your round-trip will end with a wonderful view of the antique carousel as well as geese swimming in the shallow lake waters.

CONTACT: **fairfaxcounty.gov/parks/accotink**

DIRECTIONS

From Washington, D.C., take I-395 south. Take Exit 2B/Edsall Road and travel northwest 1 mile. Turn left onto Backlick Road. After 0.4 mile, the third right, turn onto Leesville Blvd. Turn left onto Heming Ave. after 1.3 miles. Turn right into Lake Accotink Park at 0.6 mile.

Take advantage of the bird-watching opportunities by the lake.

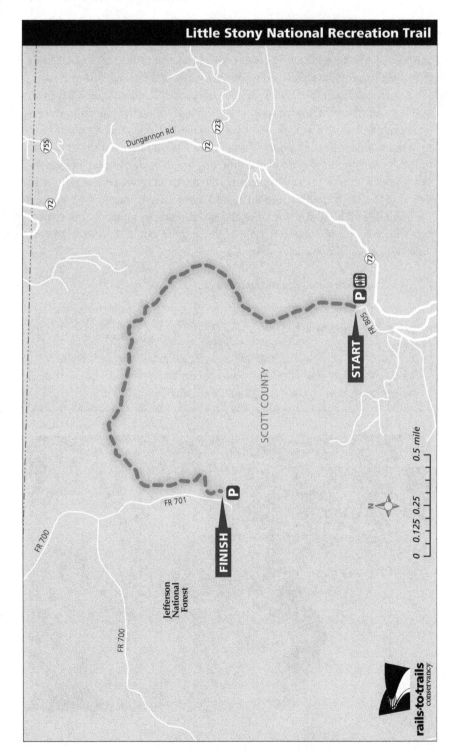

I f you're looking for an easy trip, the Little Stony National Recreation Trail in Jefferson National Forest is the perfect alternative to the nearby Devil's Fork Loop (see page 73). Devil's Fork Loop is gorgeous, but it includes a strenuous and often wet climb. Little Stony, on the other hand, offers similarly beautiful views within a mere 2.8 miles, and its footbridges save you from cold, slippery water crossings. You can also take breaks from the trail's 600-foot ascent by resting at the bridges high above the rushing currents and below the hemlock canopy.

Starting at Hanging Rock Picnic Area, follow the yellow blazes marking the route, which snakes along Little Stony Creek. The path is rather narrow in areas where it climbs in elevation and travels over boulders, and the slope is steep for a rail-trail, but the exhilarating views are worth

County
Scott

Endpoints
Forest Road 805 to Forest Road 701 (Jefferson National Forest)

Mileage
2.8

Type
Rail-Trail

Roughness Index
3

Surface
Dirt

Mountain laurel is a common plant along the path.

every step. Within 0.5-mile of the northern trailhead, you will find a viewing platform across from a 40-foot waterfall. Thick, waxy leaves of rhododendrons and mountain laurels frame the white veil of water, and if you visit in May or June, you'll likely catch the spectacular blooms of these plants. Continue uphill to find two more impressive waterfalls. Several hundred feet beyond these, you will arrive at the Little Stony Falls parking area, where the 16-mile Chief Benge Scout Trail picks up from Forest Road 701.

CONTACT: **www.fs.usda.gov/gwj**

DIRECTIONS

To access the Hanging Rock Picnic Area from Alt. US 58 in Coeburn, head south on VA 72. Travel approximately 9 miles, and turn right onto Forest Road 805 into the Hanging Rock Picnic Area. A sign marks the trailhead.

The upper trailhead, north of Hanging Rock, is a bit more complicated to find. Fortunately, the forest roads that you need to take are peppered with signs to Little Stony Falls. From the junction of VA 72 south and Alt. US 58 in Coeburn, travel south on VA 72 for 3.2 miles to VA Secondary 664. Turn right (west) onto VA 664 and go about 1 mile to Forest Road 700. Turn left onto FR 700 and continue for 1.3 miles. Then make a slight left onto FR 701, and follow it 0.8 mile to the trailhead.

Tucked in the Jefferson National Forest, this trail crisscrosses the Little Stony Creek and passes a 40-foot waterfall.

29 Mount Vernon Trail

The 18-mile Mount Vernon Trail is one of the Washington, D.C., metro area's most popular trails. Just across the Potomac River from D.C. in Virginia, the trail links Theodore Roosevelt Island Park with George Washington's estate in Mount Vernon. The trail follows the course of the Potomac, passing through parks, yacht clubs, wetlands, neighborhoods, towns, and wooded acres.

The route is mostly paved, but some sections are boardwalk. In many places, the winding path is narrow, and because it is heavily used (especially on weekends), all recreationists—whether on foot, skates, or bike—must use caution when passing others and when entering the trail from any of its numerous access points. Cyclists must dismount at some bridge crossings.

At the northern end of the trail, at the parking lot for Roosevelt Island, you can explore the island park's loop

While the destination is a worthy one, the journey along the Mount Vernon Trail is just as rewarding.

Counties
Arlington, Alexandria, Fairfax

Endpoints
US 29 and George Washington Memorial Pkwy. (Rosslyn) to Mount Vernon Estate at George Washington Memorial Pkwy. (Mount Vernon)

Mileage
18

Type
Greenway/Non-Rail-Trail

Roughness Index
1

Surface
Asphalt, Boardwalk

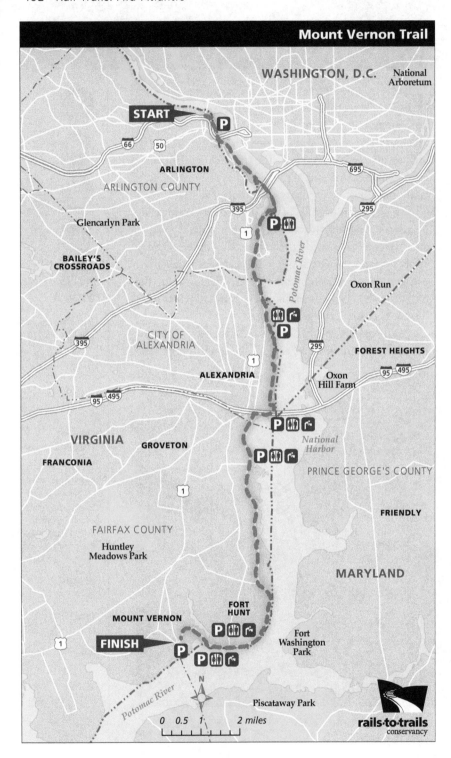

Mount Vernon Trail

WASHINGTON, D.C.   National Arboretum

START

ARLINGTON

ARLINGTON COUNTY

66   50

395

Glencarlyn Park

BAILEY'S CROSSROADS

395

CITY OF ALEXANDRIA

ALEXANDRIA

1

95 495

VIRGINIA   GROVETON

FRANCONIA

1

FAIRFAX COUNTY

Huntley Meadows Park

695

295

Potomac River

Oxon Run

295

FOREST HEIGHTS

Oxon Hill Farm   95 495

National Harbor

PRINCE GEORGE'S COUNTY

FRIENDLY

MARYLAND

FORT HUNT

MOUNT VERNON

FINISH

Fort Washington Park

1

Potomac River

N

0   0.5   1   2 miles

Piscataway Park

rails-to-trails
conservancy

trail via a footbridge over the river. Also from here, you can take a pedestrian bridge over the road and pick up the Custis Trail, which leads to the Washington & Old Dominion Trail (see page 121).

At the midpoint of the Mount Vernon Trail, navigating Old Town Alexandria can be tricky. You have two routes from which to choose, both of which are on-street. From north to south, one route follows East Abingdon Drive to Bashford Lane (where you go left, or east) to Royal Street. Or you can simply ride along George Washington Memorial Parkway/Washington Street and pick up the trail again south of I-95/I-495 (on the river side of the road). The other route, preferred by some, veers to the left (coming from the north) and continues on Union Street. From here, you have easy access to Alexandria's waterfront parks, restaurants, and shops. The marina boardwalk area is lively with all kinds of entertainment year-round, but mainly between Memorial Day and Labor Day. You can return to the trail less than a mile later at the end of Union Street near the nice townhomes along the river.

Approaching the Woodrow Wilson Bridge (I-95/I-495), you can detour east across the Potomac River (on a wide, paved trail flanking the northern side of the bridge) to reach National Harbor in Maryland. Here, you'll find dozens of shops and restaurants, not to mention the occasional waterside entertainment (water-ski shows and boating events). Otherwise, continue under the Woodrow Wilson Bridge to take the trail through more parks, marshlands, and tidy neighborhoods.

As you near the Mount Vernon Estate, the trail begins a steep climb through the forest, where it ends in the parking lot for the estate grounds. On a hot summer day, you can slake your thirst at the visitor center and rest in the shade of the trees.

CONTACT: nps.gov/gwmp/planyourvisit/mtvernontrail.htm

DIRECTIONS

You can access the Mount Vernon Trail from numerous places along its route. The three main access points are listed below.

Theodore Roosevelt Island: Access via the northbound lane only of the George Washington Memorial Pkwy. Parking can be limited on weekends. From Washington, D.C., take I-66 W to the US 50/Arlington Blvd./George Washington Memorial Pkwy. exit. Keep right and merge onto George Washington Memorial Pkwy. Take the first exit to the parking lot for Mount Vernon Trail.

Old Town Alexandria: From I-495, take Exit 177B–177C and merge onto Church St. Take an immediate left onto Washington St. and then an immediate right onto Green St. After 0.2 mile, turn right onto Royal St. and take the first left onto Jones Point Dr. (Jones Point Park). Or take I-395 to Exit 5/King St./VA 7 and head east (south) for 3.8 miles. Turn right onto Royal St., and follow it for 0.7 mile. Turn left onto Jones Point Dr. (Jones Point Park), and follow it to the parking lot. The trail runs along the river.

Mount Vernon Estate: From Arlington, take George Washington Memorial Pkwy. south about 16.7 miles to Mount Vernon Estate, which is on your left.

The Mount Vernon Trail is also accessible from Washington, D.C., Metro stations on the Blue and Orange Lines. The National Park Service website has more information, or you can visit the Washington Metropolitan Area Transit Authority (**wmata.com**).

Mount Vernon is known for its cherry blossoms.

Southern Virginia's New River Trail is one of America's premier rail-trails; the U.S. Department of the Interior designated it as an official National Recreation Trail in 2002. It is also a state park. The highlight and namesake of this magnificent trail is the 36-mile section running through Grayson, Carroll, Wythe, and Pulaski Counties along the New River, the oldest river in the United States. In 1986, the Norfolk Southern Railroad donated this old railroad corridor, which originally served to supply the once-expanding iron industry, to the Commonwealth of Virginia.

If you travel from Galax or Fries and head north, the mileage markers count down, beginning at the 57-mile marker. Also, much of the trail is downhill from south to north. If you start from Pulaski (Dora Junction), the first 3 miles are uphill, though most won't find it a burdensome climb. A mile or so before Draper, the route leads

Counties
Carroll, Grayson, Pulaski, Wythe

Endpoints
US 221/US 58 and Chestnut Creek (Galax) to Main St./VA 99 and Xaloy Way (Pulaski) with a spur to Riverview Ave. (Fries)

Mileage
57

Type
Rail-Trail

Roughness Index
1.5

Surface
Crushed Stone

This tunnel is just south of Fries Junction on the way to Galax.

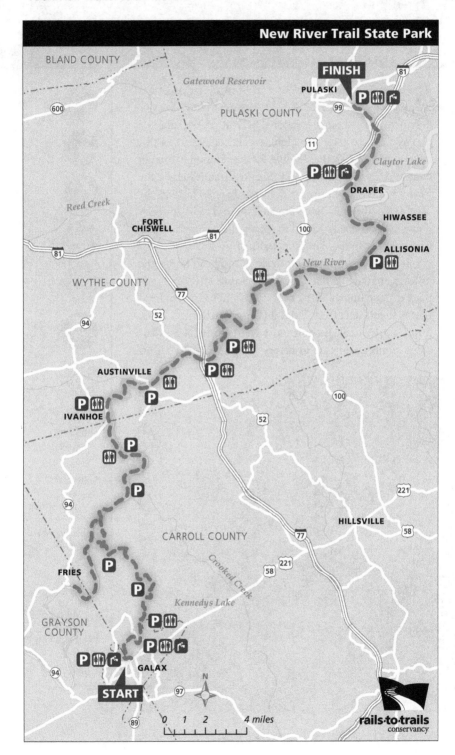

New River Trail State Park

downhill to the Hiwassee trestle at the river. This 5-mile section also features numerous trestles while offering a look into mountain railroading: The tracks climbed away from the river to reach the main line at Pulaski.

The Galax trailhead, which features an old red caboose, has plenty of parking. From here, you follow Chestnut Creek along the 12-mile Galax to Fries Junction section. The creek affords rugged scenery from the narrow valley it carved on its way to the river. At mile marker 38, you'll encounter the beautiful Fries Junction trestle bridge crossing the New River. Just across the bridge, you have the option of taking a pleasant excursion to Fries, a 12-mile round-trip. This 6-mile spur is included in the trail's 57-mile total length. The remaining 38 miles proceed north (downgrade with the river) along the peacefully flowing New River as it runs through Foster Falls, Ivanhoe, and Allisonia. The route is isolated for much of this journey; if you are on this stretch, be sure to carry all necessary supplies in case of an emergency or if you need to make a quick bike repair.

Along the way, you'll see many railroading highlights, including cavernous tunnels, steep dams, the historical shot tower (once used to make ammunition), and trestle bridges (you'll marvel at the impressive 950-foot Hiwassee trestle around mile marker 8). Both endpoints (Galax and Pulaski) have all your post-trail amenities.

CONTACT: **dcr.virginia.gov/state-parks/new-river-trail.shtml**

DIRECTIONS

To the Galax trailhead, take I-77 to the US 221/US 58 exit (Exit 14) toward Hillsville/Galax. Follow US 221 S/US 58 W for 10.1 miles. The trailhead is located on the right, where US 221/US 58 crosses Chestnut Creek.

To reach the Dora Junction trailhead in Pulaski from I-81, take Exit 94. Travel on VA 99 north for 1.6 miles toward Xaloy. Turn right onto Xaloy Way, and look for the trailhead on the right.

You can also access the trail in Fries: Take I-77 to the US 221/US 58 exit (Exit 14) toward Hillsville/Galax. Follow US 221 S/US 58 W for 7.4 miles, and turn right onto Cranberry Road/VA 722. Take the first left onto Glendale Road/VA 887. At 1.5 miles, turn right at Cliffview Road/VA 721 to Fries. At 2 miles, turn right, and then take an immediate left. VA 721 becomes Fries Road before crossing the New River at 2.2 miles from the last turn. Follow VA 606 into town (about a mile), and continue on Main St. for 0.9 mile. Turn left onto Riverview Ave. The trailhead is at the bottom of the hill; the signs are impossible to miss. Parking is available near the town park on Riverview Ave.

A parking fee is required for these lots.

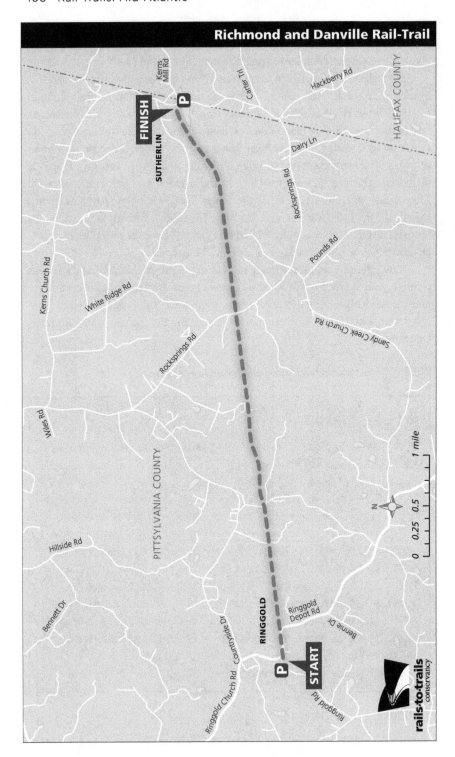

Richmond and Danville Rail-Trail

31 Richmond and Danville Rail-Trail

The Richmond and Danville Rail-Trail follows part of the right-of-way of the old railroad of the same name, an important transportation corridor for the Confederacy during the Civil War. The railroad linked the Confederate capital of Richmond with Southside, the area between the James River and the North Carolina border, where hospitals, prisons, and supply depots were located. Jefferson Davis and the Confederate Army took the route of this railroad line when they retreated from Richmond near the end of the war. They also used it to carry war supplies and Union prisoners. Today, 5.5 miles of this historical corridor, which eventually became part of the Norfolk Southern Railway system, is the scenic Richmond and Danville Rail-Trail, opened in January 2001.

Also called the Ringgold Trail, it travels past farmlands and through light woods, providing a flat route for a walk or bike ride in the rural Virginia countryside on the outskirts of Danville.

Autumn is the perfect season for a cruise along the Richmond and Danville Rail-Trail.

County
Pittsylvania

Endpoints
Ringgold Church Road and Ringgold Road (Ringgold) to Kerns Church Road/CR 948 and Railroad Trl./CR 943 (Sutherlin)

Mileage
5.5

Type
Rail-Trail

Roughness Index
2

Surface
Crushed Stone

Start your trip at the western trailhead, and in only 1 mile, you will reach a wetland area with prime waterfowl watching. This part of the ride is comfortable for bicyclists and easy for hikers of all ages; it's also wheelchair accessible. If you're looking for evidence of the area's railroading past, the eastern trailhead has a restored railroad depot and an old red caboose.

CONTACT: **pittsylvaniacountyva.gov**

DIRECTIONS

From Danville, take Bus. US 58 east for 1.5 miles and continue straight on US 58 for another 3.2 miles. Then head north (left) on CR 734/Ringgold Road for 2.1 miles. The western trailhead is located on the south side of Ringgold Road.

To access the eastern trailhead from Danville, take Bus. US 58 east for 1.5 miles and continue east on US 58/US 360 for an additional 9.2 miles. Then head north (left) on VA 656/Hackberry Road for 3.25 miles. The trailhead is west of Hackberry Road/Kerns Church Road near the intersection of Kerns Mill Road.

T he 7.5-mile paved Riverwalk Trail is part of Danville's expanding network of trails. This scenic pathway along the Dan River connects industry, beautiful parks, and natural areas. It travels through some of the most important and historical Civil War regions of southern Virginia.

Throughout the Civil War, Danville functioned as a staging area for many battles. Some of its old tobacco warehouses were turned into Civil War prisons, and the city was the last capital of the Confederate States of America after Richmond was captured by the Union Army. The trail's recommended starting point is at the Crossing at the Dan trailhead in historical downtown Danville, alongside a renovated tobacco warehouse and the active Amtrak station located on the campus of the Science Center. From here, you'll cross the Dan River on a restored 1856 railroad bridge. Once on the other side, you can go east or

The Riverwalk Trail will take you through many beautiful natural areas.

County
Danville

Endpoints
Riverside Dr. near Central Blvd., Bridge St. near Colquhoun St., and Stinson Dr. at Airport Dr. (Danville)

Mileage
7.5

Type
Rail-Trail

Roughness Index
1

Surface
Asphalt, Concrete, Boardwalk

Riverwalk Trail

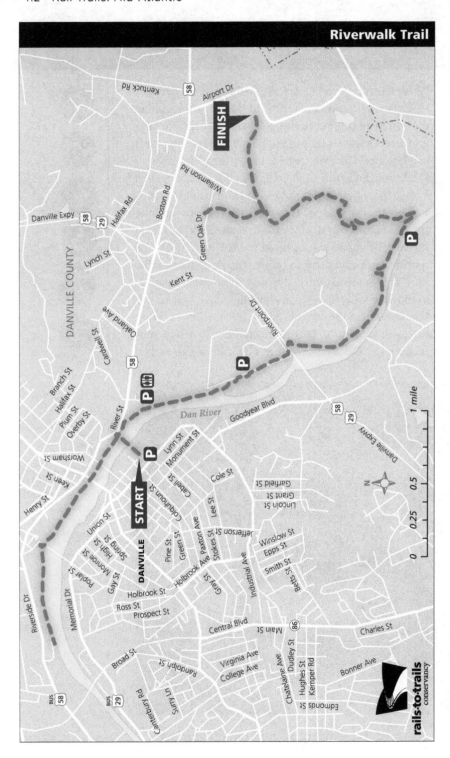

west. If you turn left (west), the trail follows the river upstream for about 1 mile until it reaches the beautiful overlook at Union Street Bridge and then continues farther upstream with access to businesses and restaurants. However, the best part of the route lies to the right, on the eastern side. From here, the riverside path will take you on an enjoyable trip through the many beautiful parks and natural areas adjacent to the Dan River. You'll see a variety of wildlife, including a goose or two, using the trail themselves.

Once you pass Dan Daniel Memorial Park, the trail continues to wind along the river through Anglers' Park. At the Anglers' Park trailhead, you have the option of continuing on the trail segment toward Danville Regional Airport. Though the terrain is hilly from here to the airport, it is the most secluded section of the Riverwalk. It links to the intertwining 25-mile Anglers Ridge single-track mountain bike trail system.

CONTACT: **playdanvilleva.com/264/riverwalk-trail**

DIRECTIONS

To reach the Crossing at the Dan, from Bus. US 58 in downtown Danville, take Main St. south across the Dan River and make the first left onto Memorial Dr., which almost immediately becomes Craghead St. Follow that for about five blocks (about 0.5 mile) until you see signs for the train station on the left. The trailhead will be on the far side of the parking lot.

Parking is also available at Dan Daniel Memorial Park, 302 River Park Dr. Take Bus. US 58 to US 29/Danville Expy./US 58, and turn right. After 1 mile, take the River Park Dr. exit. Turn right and continue for less than 0.5 mile, when the road meets the trailhead and the river.

Another access point is Anglers' Park at 350 Northside Dr. Follow the directions to Dan Daniel Memorial Park, but at the exit, take a left onto Riverpoint Dr. Follow it 0.5 mile, and turn right onto Stinson Dr. Take the first left onto Northside Dr. After 0.5 mile, turn left. The parking lot will be on your right in 0.4 mile.

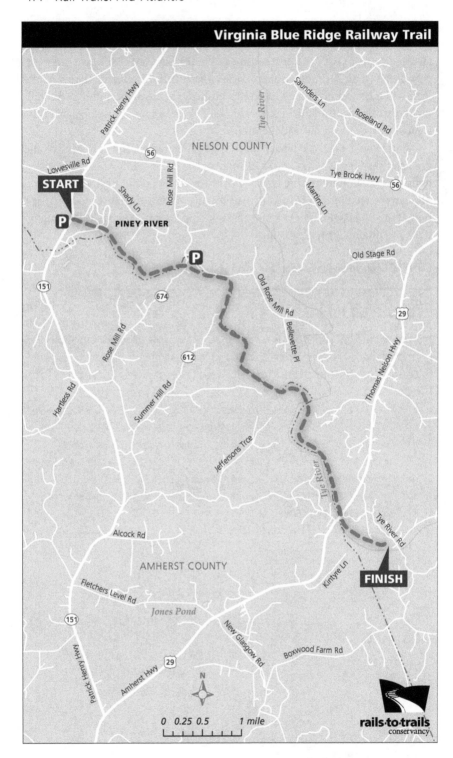

Virginia Blue Ridge Railway Trail

33 Virginia Blue Ridge Railway Trail

The 6.9-mile Virginia Blue Ridge Railway Trail begins at VA 151 in Piney River, crosses over the Naked Creek Bridge, and then carries on to pass beneath US 29 and end at Tye River Depot. Note that there is no exit at the south (Tye River Depot) end of the route, so trail-goers will need to turn around. You can also access the trail at Roses Mill. Portable toilets are available at the Piney River trailhead. During the autumn hunting season, trail users should wear blaze orange clothing.

The Virginia Blue Ridge Railway Trail offers a quint-essential rail-trail experience in central Virginia, midway between Lynchburg and Charlottesville (less than an hour's drive from each). The scenic route follows along the Piney and Tye Rivers, where wildflowers bloom from spring through summer, and white-tailed deer and other wild-life abound. The trail occupies the railbed of the former

The scales and tip car at mile 6.9

Counties
Amherst, Nelson

Endpoints
Patrick Henry Hwy./VA 151 (Piney River) to Tye River Depot (Arrington)

Mileage
6.9

Type
Rail-Trail

Roughness Index
1

Surface
Asphalt, Ballast, Crushed Stone

Virginia Blue Ridge Railway, which ran from Tye River Depot (to interchange with the Southern Railway) to Massies Mill until it fell into disuse in 1980.

The route is an easy, picturesque ride through a beautiful, natural setting with plentiful opportunities to see unique historical sites. The Piney and Tye Rivers are constant companions, and you'll cross five bridges on the route, including a photo-worthy covered bridge at Naked Creek.

Begin your journey at the northern trailhead in Piney River, where a renovated depot serves as a visitor center, and explore the new Historic Railroad Park. The railbed on which the rail-trail now rests was originally built in 1915 to haul timber to local mills. Much of the crushed stone trail travels through wooded areas, offering a cool respite even during the hot summer months. The trail also passes through farm country and open fields. Along your journey, you'll see other relics of the past, such as rail cars and a railroad weighing scale on display. The trail ends at the Tye River Depot, where you will turn around and head back to Piney River.

CONTACT: blueridge-railtrail.org

DIRECTIONS

To access the Piney River trailhead (at 3124 Patrick Henry Hwy.) from Lynchburg, take US 29 N 16.2 miles to VA 151. Turn left, and follow VA 151/Patrick Henry Hwy. for 6.8 miles to the trailhead. From Charlottesville, take US 29 S for 33.7 miles to VA 56 at Colleen. Turn right onto VA 56, and travel 5 miles to turn left onto VA 151. After 1.2 miles, you'll see the trailhead sign on the left. Parking for cars and horse trailers is available, as well as portable toilets.

To access the Roses Mill trailhead, take US 29 to VA 56 at Colleen; turn onto VA 56 W and go about 4 miles. Turn left onto Roses Mill Road/VA 674. The trailhead is about 1.4 miles farther (around milepost 1.8 of the trail).

34 Virginia Creeper National Recreation Trail

The Virginia Creeper National Recreation Trail offers scenic wonders: from dense forests, open fields, and lush waterways to railroad relics and delightful small towns. Cyclists and equestrians love the length of the Creeper, and many local walkers and joggers take advantage of the pleasant opportunity for a little exercise.

The route officially begins at the Virginia–North Carolina border, but the easiest place to start the Creeper is from the Whitetop trailhead. (However, to cover the entire trail, simply ride the extra mile from Whitetop to the North Carolina border before turning around to begin your journey.)

The first 17-mile stretch to Damascus allows for numerous restroom breaks at its many trailheads, some of which are housed in restored or replica railroad depots. This section travels through terrific scenery, from

This trail was inducted into the Rail-Trail Hall of Fame in 2014.

Counties
Grayson, Washington

Endpoints
Green Spring Road and Pecan St. (Abingdon) to VA 726/Whitetop Gap Road (Whitetop)

Mileage
34

Type
Rail-Trail

Roughness Index
2

Surface
Gravel

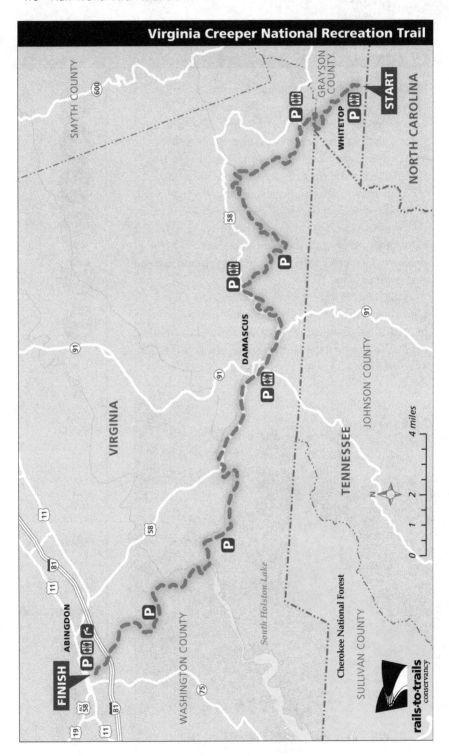

Virginia Creeper National Recreation Trail

Christmas tree farms and grazing llamas to river views and deep forestland. The Appalachian Trail also weaves on and off the Creeper. After going through dense trees, you will emerge to glide over bridges high above Laurel and Green Cove Creeks.

Around the midpoint of the Virginia Creeper Trail, you'll reach the Damascus trailhead. Before tackling the rest of the trail, consider taking a break in this sweet town. Damascus is the self-proclaimed friendliest town on the trail, and it won't take you long to see why: Here, you'll find restrooms, a caboose housing an information booth, a replica train engine, and parking. Veer off the trail to find lunch stops and bike shops in town.

After your break, get ready for a little work; from Damascus to the trail's end in Abingdon, a little more effort is required. The constant downhill is exchanged for a flat grade with some gentle rises and descents. It's not strenuous, but it is a change from the first section. If you are bicycling, be aware that abundant equestrian use just after Damascus can leave its mark on the trail surface and give you a bumpy ride. But don't let a few bumps get you down. They start to peter out about 7 miles before Abingdon, and some of the Creeper's most beautiful river and farmland views are still ahead.

On a ridgeline high above the South Fork of the Holston River, you will emerge onto a bridge offering invigorating views of South Holston Lake below. As you continue your journey toward Abingdon, you will run into cattle gates across the trail. These gates mark your entrance to the Creeper's expansive grazing meadows. This tranquil farmland accompanies you for much of the remainder of the journey.

About a half mile from Abingdon is a public park with restrooms, picnic areas, and a water fountain. Just across the last bridge, you will reach the endpoint. If you are traveling to the Virginia Creeper from out of town, consider that many bike shops in Damascus and Abingdon offer bike rentals and a shuttle to the Whitetop trailhead.

CONTACT: **vacreepertrail.org**

DIRECTIONS

To get to the Whitetop trailhead, take I-81 to Exit 19 (Abingdon/Damascus). Turn right (east) and follow US 58 10.7 miles into Damascus. Continue on US 58 by turning right and following it another 16.4 miles. Turn right onto VA 726/Whitetop Gap Road, and head south toward the North Carolina border. After 1.5 miles, you will see the parking area off of VA 726.

To get to the Abingdon trailhead, take I-81 to Exit 17. Head north on Alt. US 58/Cummings St. for 0.2 mile. Turn right onto Green Spring Road, and follow it for 0.5 mile. A large locomotive engine is on display by the trailhead, which you can see across from the parking lot.

Green Cove Station, the only original depot building remaining along the Virginia Creeper Trail

35 Washington & Old Dominion Regional Park

The Washington & Old Dominion Trail (W&OD) is one of suburban Washington, D.C.'s most popular rail-trails. The heavily used trail is frequented by commuters and recreationists alike, and it is a fantastic link between Virginia's rural and historical past and the nation's capital.

The W&OD Railroad was built on the eve of the Civil War in 1858. At times both a passenger line and a freight line, the railroad eventually lost out to more efficient modes of transportation and went into disuse in 1968. In 1982, the Northern Virginia Parks Association bought the right-of-way and maintains the trail today with the help of volunteers from Friends of the W&OD.

The route is exceptionally well marked, with posts indicating every 0.5 mile. The trail begins in the Shirlington section of Arlington, Virginia, at a nicely conceived information area that features a drinking fountain (summers

The Washington & Old Dominion Trail is the premiere rail-trail of Northern Virginia and a member of the Rail-Trail Hall of Fame.

Counties
Arlington, Fairfax, Loudoun

Endpoints
Four Mile Run Dr. and Shirlington Rd. (Arlington) to 21st St./VA 690 (Purcellville)

Mileage
45

Type
Rail-Trail

Roughness Index
1

Surface
Asphalt, Concrete

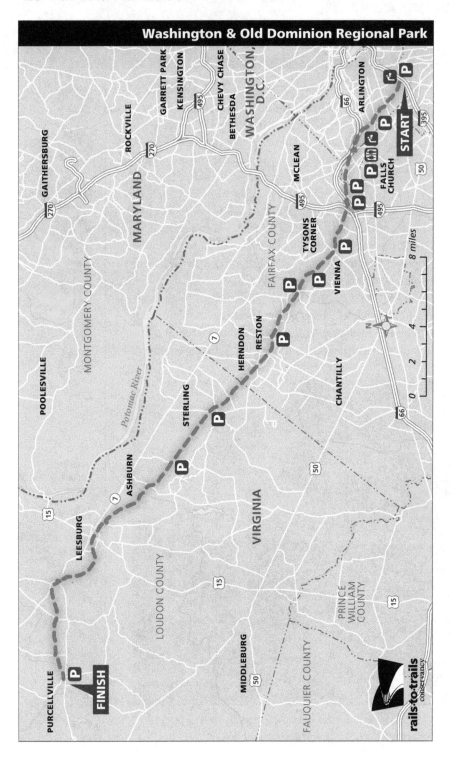

Washington & Old Dominion Regional Park

only) and interpretive signs. In fact, you'll find interpretive signs scattered all along the route, each telling the story of the people and places along the rail line. This part of Shirlington is a nice starting or ending point; just a few blocks away is a nicely revitalized shopping and dining district with a movie theater, as well as the Signature Theatre for the live variety. In addition, if you want to head into D.C. from here, just cross Shirlington Road and pick up the Four Mile Run Trail.

On the W&OD Trail from Shirlington, the route is quite urban for a few miles, but you soon leave trappings of the city behind to enter leafier suburbs. From east to west, the trail does gain elevation, albeit gradually. However, if you start in Purcellville and head to Shirlington, you won't have to pedal so hard. Bluemont Park (at 3.5 miles) is one of many picnic areas and parks within the trail's first 10 miles; it's a great rest stop and has both water and restrooms. You'll also find an old caboose here, one of many along the way, as well as a link to the Bluemont Junction Trail, constructed on a former spur line of the W&OD Railroad.

At 5.5 miles, the trail provides access to Washington's Metrorail system on the Orange and Silver Lines via the East Falls Church Station. As you continue to make your way beyond the I-495 Beltway, use caution at all road crossings, especially during rush hour. In Fairfax County, the path continues through the communities of Vienna (mile 12 and with an old caboose and train depot) and Reston (mile 18). Both towns offer plenty of off-trail shops and restaurants for a nice break or diversion. The suburban neighborhoods surrounding the trail become more wooded too. Halfway between Vienna and Reston, a worthwhile side trip is the beautiful Meadowlark Botanical Gardens. The mile-long Meadowlark Connector Trail, which connects directly with the W&OD Trail, will take you there.

The town of Herndon (at mile 20.5) has a trailside train depot used as a visitor center and also another caboose. As the trail continues, it passes through Sterling (mile 23) and Ashburn (mile 27.5), where enterprising folks are known to set up trailside barbecue stands between spring and autumn. The historical town of Leesburg (mile 34), a popular spot for lunch and antiquing, has a Colonial feel. The trail also passes through a nice park, and from here west, it begins to take on a more rural tone.

The final 10 miles from Leesburg to Purcellville travel through rolling hills of Virginia Piedmont farmland. Horses graze, cornfields flourish, and trail crowds thin out somewhat. The route ends at the Purcellville Train Depot (mile 44.8), which features restaurants and a bike shop for your trail-riding needs.

CONTACT: **wodfriends.org** or **nvrpa.org/park/w_od_railroad**

DIRECTIONS

To begin at the southern end of the W&OD Trail, from I-395 N, take Exit 6 (Shirlington). Exit right onto S. Shirlington Road. In 0.2 mile, at the second traffic light, arrive at S. Four Mile Run Dr. The W&OD Trail parallels the road. You can park along the side of the road, but it is not advisable to leave your car overnight here. In fact, you're better off parking in one of the parking garages just across the road in downtown Shirlington.

To begin at the northern end in Purcellville, take VA 7 W for 30 miles. Exit at VA 287 and turn left. Follow VA 287 for 0.7 mile, and turn right onto Bus. VA 7. After 1.3 miles, turn right again onto 23rd St., which becomes 21st St. The Purcellville Train Depot is 0.25 mile away on the right. Parking is across the street, but there are time limits during certain days of the week. Unlimited parking time is permitted at a small lot one block east along the trail off Hatcher Ave. Parking and trail access are available in dozens of places along the route; see **wodfriends.org.**

36 Wilderness Road Trail

History runs deep along the Wilderness Road Trail, which roughly follows a path carved by Daniel Boone in April 1775. The path later became a route on the Louisville & Nashville Railroad before finally being converted to a rail-trail that stretches from a national historical park to a state park.

At the western trailhead in Cumberland Gap National Historical Park, the Wilderness Road Trail connects to the 1.6-mile Boone Trail, which links to a larger trail system that continues through the Cumberland Gap. Just beyond the trailhead in Cumberland Gap National Historical Park, you might catch a glimpse of buffalo grazing in a privately owned, fenced area.

The first 2 miles run right next to US 58. Though this sounds unpleasant, you are separated from vehicles, and there is something soothing about riding through forsythia toward forest and farmland. After this stretch, the trail backs into a quiet and much more scenic area behind a veil of trees, though the path still parallels US 58 until the trail's

County
Lee

Endpoints
Old Wilderness Road/
US 58 (TN–VA state line)
to Daniel Boone Trail/
US 58 (near Ewing)

Mileage
8.5

Type
Rail-Trail

Roughness Index
2

Surface
Crushed Stone

Despite being close to civilization, the Wilderness Road Trail is the ultimate escape.

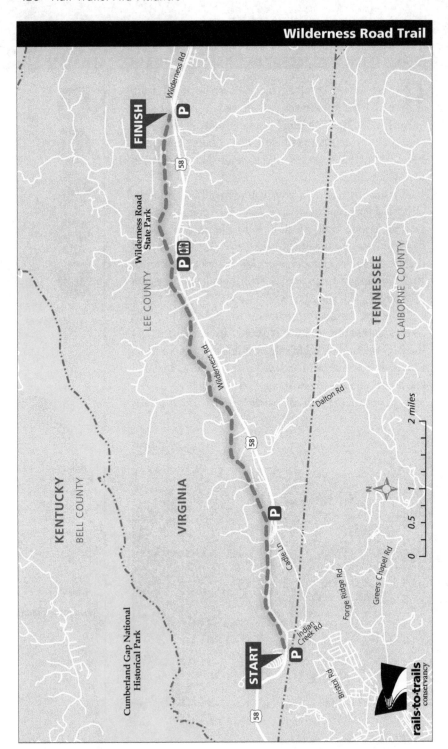

terminus just west of Ewing. Once it retreats from the road, the route meanders through nearly 7 miles of picturesque farmland, complete with bright white fences and grazing cattle. The trail is dotted with quaint homes, barns, and silos, and the impressive Cumberland Mountain serves as a backdrop to this idyllic landscape.

Wilderness Road State Park hosts reenactments and living history events throughout the year. The Joseph Martin House, located in the park and next to the trail, offers restrooms, a gift shop, and local history exhibits. There is a user fee to enter the park.

CONTACT: dcr.virginia.gov/state-parks/wilderness-road.shtml

DIRECTIONS

To reach the westernmost trailhead in Cumberland Gap from Abingdon, take I-81 S about 18.5 miles to Exit 1, and head west on US 421/US 58/Gate City Hwy. for 24.2 miles. Near Gate City, turn right onto US 23/US 421/US 58, and continue for 17.8 miles. Near Duffield, turn left onto US 58/Duff-Patt Road, and travel 19.8 miles. In Jonesville, turn left to stay on US 58 and continue another 30.7 miles (4 miles west of Wilderness Road State Park, you will pass a gazebo and paved lot, and the trailhead is 2 miles past that). The trail's start point is off of US 58, and you'll find limited roadside parking there. If you're coming from the west on US 58, the trailhead is about 2 miles east of the intersection of US 58 and US 25.

The easternmost trailhead is also right off of US 58 at a paved parking lot about 3 miles west of Ewing. If you're heading west on US 58 from Abingdon, you'll see a sign stating that Cumberland Gap is 10 miles away. The parking area is on the north side of US 58.

End your day on the trail with a visit to Wilderness Road State Park.

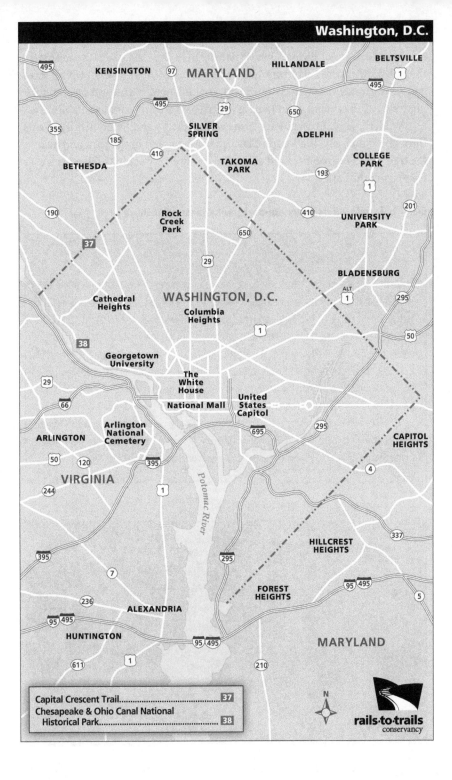

Washington, D.C.

Capital Crescent Trail **37**
Chesapeake & Ohio Canal National
   Historical Park **38**

rails·to·trails
conservancy

The Chesapeake & Ohio Canal Towpath offers spectacular scenery as it winds through Washington, D.C., and Maryland.

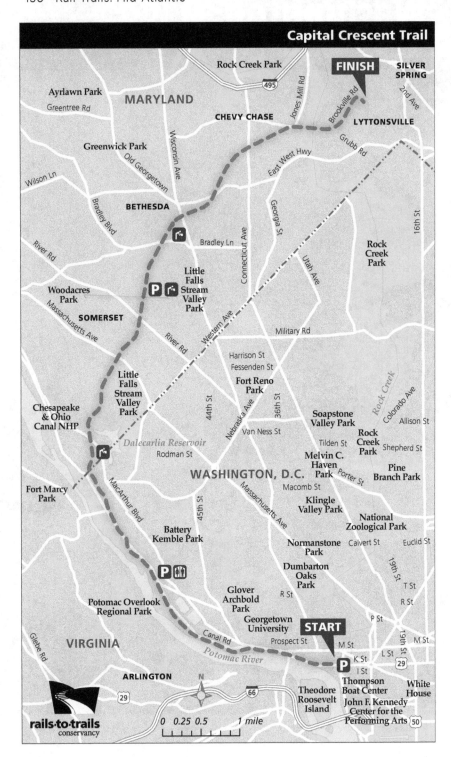

Capital Crescent Trail

37 Capital Crescent Trail

The 11-mile Capital Crescent Trail follows the route of the Baltimore & Ohio Railroad's Georgetown Branch rail line, from the heart of historic Georgetown in Washington, D.C., to Silver Spring, Maryland, east of the Rock Creek Trestle. For the 7 miles between Georgetown and Bethesda, Maryland, the Capital Crescent Trail is paved, and much of it includes an adjacent gravel trail for joggers. Between Bethesda and Lyttonsville, Maryland, the 3-mile stretch of trail is surfaced with crushed stone; this segment is called the Georgetown Branch. From Lyttonsville, the Georgetown Branch Trail continues for 2 miles as an on-road bike route into downtown Silver Spring.

Future plans call for creating a hard surface alongside the proposed Purple Line light rail between Bethesda and downtown Silver Spring, where the Capital Crescent will connect to the Metropolitan Branch Trail.

The Capital Crescent Trail is a favorite for DC dwellers looking to escape.

Counties
Montgomery (MD),
Washington (MD)

Endpoints
30th St. NW at White-
hurst Fwy. (Georgetown,
Washington, D.C.) to
Lanier Dr. at Talbot Ave.
(Silver Spring, MD)

Mileage
11

Type
Rail-Trail

Roughness Index
1

Surface
Asphalt, Crushed Stone,
Gravel

In Georgetown, the trail travels with the Potomac River on one side and the Chesapeake & Ohio Canal National Historical Park towpath on the other side. From the trail, you can watch the rowing crews of Georgetown University as they practice, or perhaps you'll jog past a senator. Deer, foxes, rabbits, many species of birds, and ubiquitous local squirrels—white, gray, and black—also share the path. In Georgetown near Thompson Boat Center, and in west Silver Spring at Jones Mill Road, the trail connects to Rock Creek Park, a densely forested area that closes many of its roads to car traffic on weekends and becomes a playground for nonmotorized uses. The loop of the Capital Crescent Trail and Rock Creek Park totals 22 miles and takes you past the National Zoological Park and the John F. Kennedy Center for the Performing Arts. In Silver Spring, Bethesda, and Georgetown, you will find a number of places immediately off the trail to have a meal or a cup of coffee, as well as a large number of retail shops.

CONTACT: cctrail.org

DIRECTIONS

To begin in the Georgetown neighborhood of Washington, D.C., go south on Wisconsin Ave. to its end under the Whitehurst Fwy. (US 29), and turn right onto Water St. NW. The trail begins at the end of Water St. NW. Parking is usually available along Water St. on weekends.

To start in Bethesda, take the Capital Beltway/I-495 to the MD 355 (Wisconsin Ave.) exit, and head south 4 miles toward Bethesda. In downtown Bethesda, turn right onto Bethesda Ave. The trail crosses Bethesda Ave. at Woodmont Ave., just one block west of Wisconsin Ave.

To reach the Silver Spring terminus from the Capital Beltway/I-495, take the Georgia Ave. exit south toward Silver Spring. After 1.5 miles, turn right onto Colesville Road in downtown Silver Spring toward the Metro station. At the first light, turn right onto Second Ave. The Georgetown Branch Trail starts at this intersection.

38 Chesapeake & Ohio Canal National Historical Park

The Chesapeake & Ohio Canal National Historical Park (also known as the C&O Canal Towpath) follows the route of the Potomac River for 184.5 miles between Georgetown in Washington, D.C., and Cumberland, Maryland. Hundreds of original features, including locks, lockhouses, aqueducts, and other canal structures, are reminders of the canal's role as a transportation system during the Canal Era, which peaked in the mid-19th century. Not to be missed is the Paw Paw Tunnel at milepost 155.2 at the northern end of the trail.

The C&O Canal Towpath was an engineering feat that, unfortunately for investors, was largely outdone by the competing railroad that parallels the towpath in many places. Today, however, recreationists of all types can enjoy this mostly level, continuous trail through the spectacular scenery of the Potomac River valley. Every

Counties
Allegany, Frederick, Montgomery, Washington (all in MD)

Endpoints
29th St. at Rock Creek Pkwy. (Georgetown, Washington, D.C.) to W. Harrison St. near I-68 (Cumberland, MD)

Mileage
184.5

Type
Canal

Roughness Index
2

Surface
Crushed Stone, Dirt, Gravel

Connecting Washington, D.C., to Cumberland, Maryland, the Chesapeake & Ohio Canal Towpath can be a relaxing stroll or a multiday adventure.

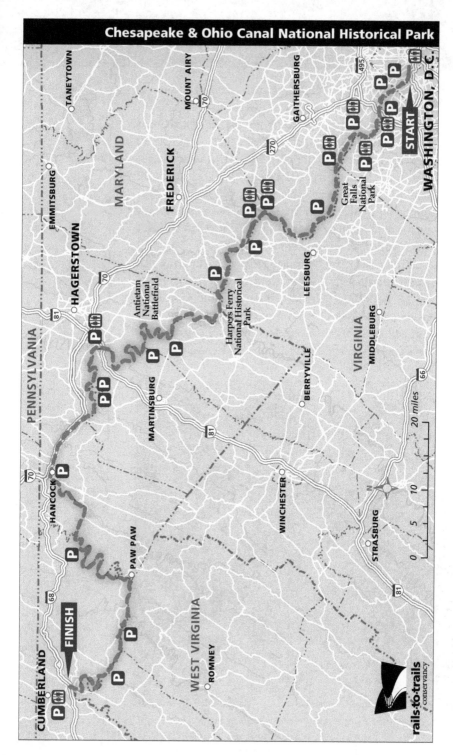

Chesapeake & Ohio Canal National Historical Park

year, millions of visitors hike or bike the C&O; the peak season is May–October. Weekends spring–fall are busy, especially around Washington, D.C., and Great Falls National Park in Maryland.

The trail provides campgrounds (both private and public), picnic areas, portable toilets, and lookout points along the way. You'll also find amenities, such as cafés and restaurants, B&Bs and motels, bike shops, museums, and retail shops, as well as innumerable historical sites. A handful of visitor centers operated by the National Park Service sell guidebooks and provide information about the towpath, its history, and local points of interest. You can even stay the night in one of a handful of restored lockhouses (visit **nps.gov/choh** for more information).

Of particular importance is the role the canal itself played during the American Civil War as a dividing line between the North and South. Troops on both sides of the conflict lobbed ammunitions across the water, crossing the river and canal numerous times to raid enemy camps, sabotage canal operations, and march to and from battles, including the Gettysburg Campaign. Though many aren't marked, several sites along the canal were the scenes of events both tragic and heroic. (Again, the National Park Service visitor centers sell books that recount these sites and events.)

Most of the trail is heavily wooded, and river views are best during early spring, late fall, and winter, when trees are leafless. Also, because the path requires regular maintenance, some sections may be closed for repairs. Visit **nps.gov/choh** for current information on trail detours.

From Cumberland, the trail connects to the Great Allegheny Passage (see page 29), where you can extend your ride all the way to Pittsburgh.

CONTACT: nps.gov/choh

DIRECTIONS

Various sections of the towpath can be reached along I-495, I-70, and I-68.

To access the trail in Cumberland, visit the Cumberland Visitor Center at the Western Maryland Railway station. From the east, take Exit 43C off I-68. At the bottom of the ramp, make a left onto Harrison St., and follow Harrison 0.1 mile to the visitor center in the Western Maryland Railway Museum.

To access the trail in Great Falls National Park in Maryland, take Exit 41 off I-495 (Carderock/Great Falls, MD), and follow Clara Barton Pkwy. for 1.7 miles. At the stop sign (at the end of the road), make a slight left onto MacArthur Blvd., and follow it for approximately 3.5 miles into the park. There is a fee at the Great Falls National Park entrance to the C&O.

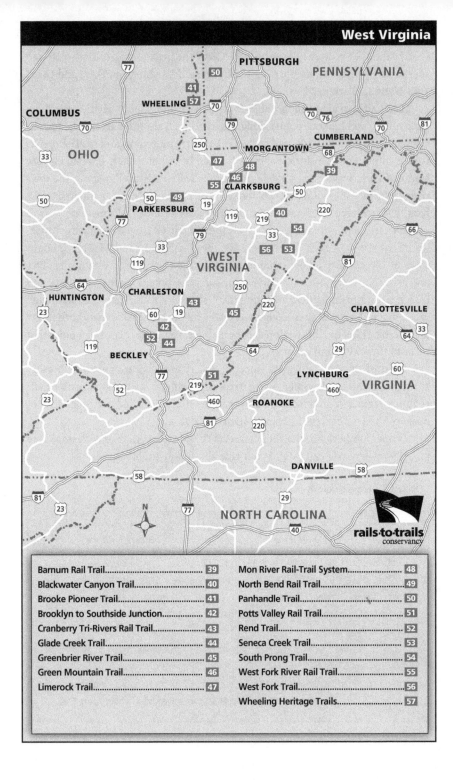

West Virginia

West Virginia

The Mon River Rail-Trails follow their namesake waterway, the beautiful Monongahela River.

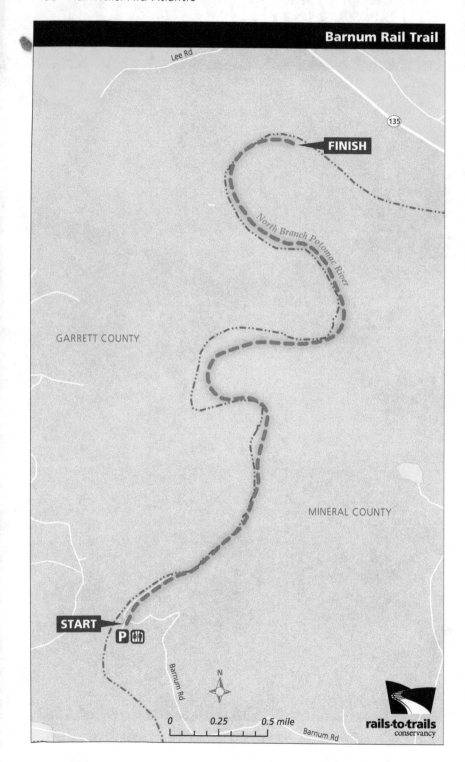

39 Barnum Rail Trail

Nestled in a northern valley of West Virginia, the Barnum Rail Trail follows the North Branch of the Potomac River through the superb scenery of the Upper Potomac region. If you plan to explore this out-and-back trail by bike, a mountain bike is the best choice for tackling the packed ballast surface.

The route begins in the very small community of Barnum, just north of Jennings Randolph Lake in Mineral County. The trailhead (the only access point for this route) is very pleasant, with ample parking, restroom facilities, and a small park overlooking the Potomac River, which offers access to incredible fishing.

Exercise caution for the first mile; the trail is open to vehicular traffic, though you probably won't encounter too many cars at this remote location. Beyond the large parking area and a closed gate, the remaining 3 miles are strictly nonmotorized.

The peaceful pathway winds through a densely wooded area.

County
Mineral

Endpoints
Barnum Road and North Branch of the Potomac River (Barnum)

Mileage
4

Type
Rail-Trail

Roughness Index
2

Surface
Ballast, Dirt, Grass

After the gate, the trail heads into the open and offers stunning views of the vibrant Potomac. Lush hillsides rise on either side of the river, and the trail hugs the west slope, while the water churns and flows immediately to your left for the next 2 miles.

The path then enters a densely wooded area—a landscape it maintains to its northern endpoint about a mile ahead. You can hear the active rapids only a few hundred feet away at any given time. Though no official signage marks the end of the trail, it becomes apparent where the corridor is no longer maintained. At this point, simply turn around and enjoy the ride or walk back.

CONTACT: mineralcountywv.com/parksandrecreation

DIRECTIONS

To access the trailhead for this out-and-back, take I-68 to Cumberland, MD, and get off at Exit 42 (US 220/Greene St./Keyser). Take US 220 S 21.7 miles through Keyser, and continue straight on WV 972 for 2.1 miles. Then head west on US 50. After 7.3 miles, take a right onto WV 42 and then, after 4.9 miles, bear right onto WV 46. Once in Cross, at 6.5 miles, take a left onto Barnum Road and follow it to the end (1.8 miles). The trail will be on the right.

The sounds of the North Branch of the Potomac River accompany a visit to the Barnum Rail Trail.

40 Blackwater Canyon Trail

In 1888, the Blackwater Canyon Trail, located in the Monongahela National Forest, was used to haul coal and lumber through this stunning canyon. Today, remnants of this history still remain just outside of Thomas in the form of coke ovens that line the trail along the mountainside.

The Blackwater Canyon Trail is perfect for hikers or mountain bikers in search of solitude. The route curves along Blackwater River and its North Branch, meandering through Blackwater Falls State Park. As such, this is a terrifically scenic pathway, with mountains lining both sides of the canyon, and the roaring river a steady sound track to your journey. The finest views of the river, including scenic waterfalls, are enjoyed during late fall, winter, and early spring, when the trees don't have as many leaves.

It is best to follow this trail from Thomas to Hendricks because there is considerable climb in the other direction.

For gorgeous waterfalls and solitude, try the Blackwater Canyon Trail.

County
Tucker

Endpoints
Main St. at Second St. (Hendricks) to Douglas Road near US 48 (Thomas)

Mileage
10.5

Type
Rail-Trail

Roughness Index
2

Surface
Dirt, Gravel

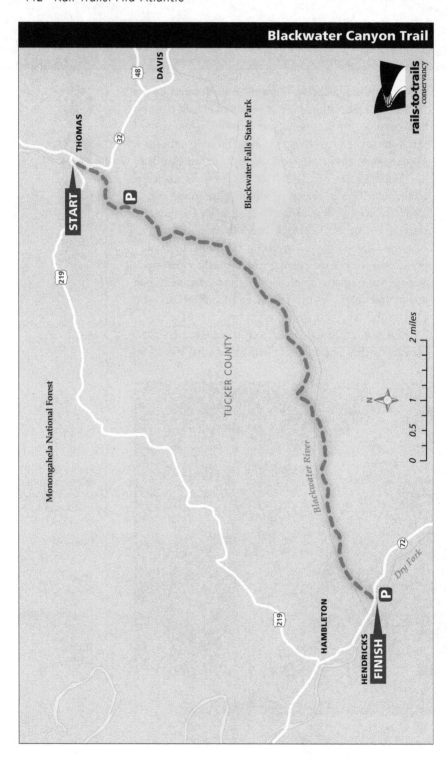

As you travel along the Blackwater Canyon Trail, you may happen upon one of several rare species, including the West Virginia northern flying squirrel (once endangered), Indiana bat (currently endangered), or the Cheat Mountain salamander (a threatened species). The habitat surrounding the trail is vital to the survival of these species, so it is important to stay on the path. In Hendricks, it is also possible to pick up the Allegheny Highlands Trail and Limerock Trail (hiking only; see page 162).

CONTACT: **www.fs.usda.gov/mnf**

DIRECTIONS

From Morgantown, take WV 7 approximately 32 miles to Terra Alta. Turn right onto N. Main St. and immediately veer left to Aurora Ave., which becomes Aurora Pike. Follow it for 10.1 miles to US 50. Head west (left) on US 50 for 1.5 miles, and turn right onto WV 24. After 5.5 miles, turn right onto US 219. Follow US 219 for 9.1 miles, and once in Thomas, head south on WV 32/Spruce St. After 0.5 mile, turn right onto Douglas Road, which crosses the trail. You will reach the trailhead approximately 1 mile down the road. The trailhead, where there is space for parking, is marked by a U.S. Forest Service gate.

From Morgantown, follow US 119 S approximately 11 miles. Turn left onto Gladesville Road; after 3 miles, turn left again to stay on Gladesville for another 3.3 miles. Turn right onto WV 92, and follow it 12 miles. Turn left onto US 50, and travel 11.5 miles. Take a sharp right onto WV 72, and take it for 20.3 miles. In Parsons, turn left onto First St., and in less than 0.5 mile, turn right to continue on WV 72/US 219. At 1.6 miles, veer right to continue on WV 72 for another 1.5 miles into Hendricks. Turn right onto Second St., and the trailhead will be on the right. Look for the gazebo and parking at the trailhead.

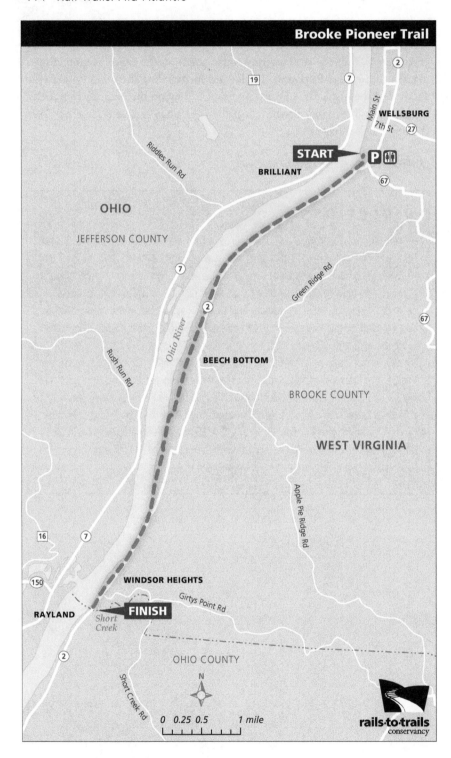

41 Brooke Pioneer Trail

Expansive interpretive signs along this route describe the local history of the Panhandle Railroad. Once called the Wheeling Secondary Track—between Weirton and Benwood, West Virginia—the line opened in 1878. Serving freight (until 1981) and passengers (until 1951), the tracks were pulled in 1987, and it would be another decade before trail construction began.

The Brooke Pioneer Trail follows the east bank of the Ohio River between Wellsburg and the Brooke–Ohio County line at Short Creek. Here, the Brooke Pioneer Trail continues into Ohio County as the Wheeling Heritage Trails (see page 200). Both paths are paved and provide a total of 18 miles of scenic hiking or biking along the river between the two cities they connect.

In the north, the Brooke Pioneer Trail begins at a connection with the Wellsburg Yankee Trail, another

County
Brooke

Endpoints
Charles St. at WV 2 (Wellsburg) to Short Creek Road at WV 2 (Short Creek)

Mileage
6.7

Type
Rail-Trail

Roughness Index
1

Surface
Asphalt

The smell of honeysuckle fills the air along the Brooke Pioneer Trail each spring.

rail-trail on the same corridor in the community's downtown. Extending south from Wellsburg, the trail crosses Buffalo Creek on a restored railroad trestle paralleling WV 2. This is how the route continues for its entire journey: wedged between the road and the Ohio River.

That doesn't mean the views are lacking. In fact, the road is often shielded from view by brush, likely there since the days of the railroad. Looking to the west, trail users are treated to stunning vistas of the powerful Ohio River and the dramatic climbs and drops of the hills in Ohio just beyond.

Those looking for reminders of the area's industrial past won't be disappointed, either. The trail skirts the edge of a handful of manufacturing properties between Wellsburg and Windsor Heights, and the large cooling tower and smokestack of Ohio's Cardinal Power Plant interrupt the views of the rolling wooded landscape on the opposite shore.

CONTACT: **brookepioneertrail.20megsfree.com/about.html**

DIRECTIONS

From Wheeling, take I-70 to Exit 1. Turn right (north) onto WV 2, and follow it for 15.3 miles to Wellsburg. Park just south of the bridge off WV 2 south of town.

To reach the Short Creek trailhead from Wheeling, take I-70 to Exit 1. Turn right (north) onto WV 2, and follow it for 8.5 miles to Short Creek. Park just south of the bridge off WV 2 at Stone Shannon Road. Use caution when crossing WV 2 to access the trail.

Limited parking is also available just off the trail in Beech Bottom, 3 miles north of Short Creek and 4 miles south of Wellsburg.

As it weaves past long-abandoned mining towns, such as Red Ash and Rush Run, the Brooklyn to Southside Junction trail (also known as the Southside Trail) tells the unique history of Appalachia's prominent coal mining industry. Once an important transportation passage used to haul coal from the remote New River Gorge, this recycled railroad corridor now brings new life into the area as a tourist attraction. Never more than 100 yards from the New River, the trail provides users with an up-close look at the natural beauty found within and along the New River Gorge National River.

A forest of large oak trees, rhododendrons, and evergreens envelops you as you travel the meandering path along the bank of the river. One of the most popular among the area's many trails, it is particularly attractive to mountain bikers who enjoy the rough riding provided by exposed railroad ties along its route.

This 6-mile trail runs along the New River, a popular rafting destination in West Virginia.

County
Fayette

Endpoints
Cunard River Access (Brooklyn) to Thurmond Road near CR 25 (Thurmond)

Mileage
6

Type
Rail-Trail

Roughness Index
2

Surface
Ballast, Dirt, Gravel

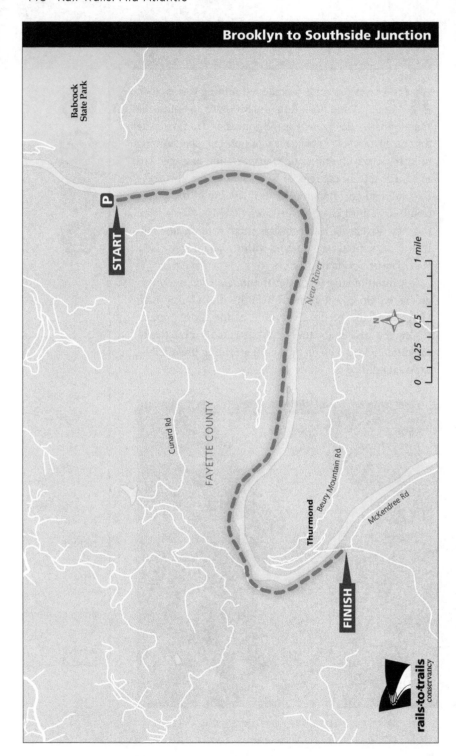

Beginning at the Brooklyn trailhead, head south along the New River. Listen for the exuberant screams of whitewater rafters on the water, one of the finest whitewater rivers in the eastern United States. Active railroad tracks at Southside Junction signal the temporary end of the trail. While the trail extends past these tracks to a trailhead at Southside Junction, a legal (and safe) crossing here is currently not available. According to the National Park Service, negotiations are under way, but in the interim, please respect this private property and keep clear of the tracks.

CONTACT: nps.gov/neri

DIRECTIONS

To reach the Brooklyn trailhead from I-64, take Exit 124/Beckley. Go north on Joe L. Smith Dr. for 0.7 mile, and turn left onto Brookshire Ln. Make an immediate right onto US 19, and follow it north for 6.2 miles. Near Prosperity, take a right to continue to follow US 19 for another 9.5 miles. Exit at Main St./WV 16 in Oak Hill. In about 0.5 mile, turn right onto Martin Ave., and then turn left onto Gatewood Ave. Follow it for 5.4 miles. Turn right at Cunard Road; at 1.8 miles, take a left onto Brooklyn Loop, and then take an immediate left. Follow the paved road 1.7 miles, veering right at intersections, to the Brooklyn trailhead, where parking is available. The Southside Junction end is not recommended as a starting point because the active rail line perpendicular to the trail often blocks access to the trailhead, making crossing hazardous.

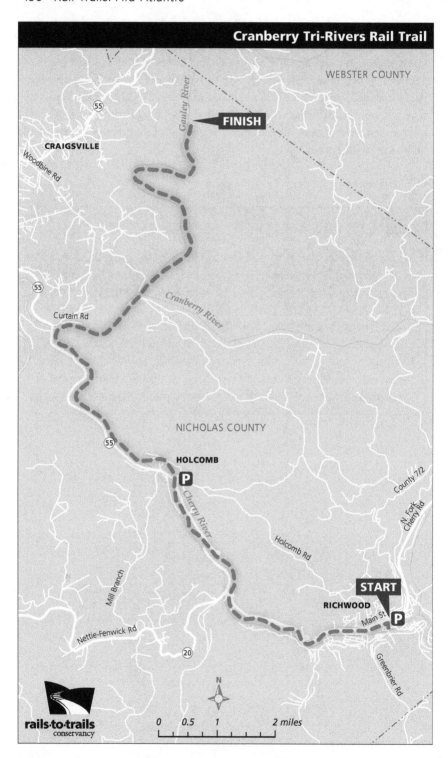

43 Cranberry Tri-Rivers Rail Trail

The Cranberry Tri-Rivers Rail Trail, also called the Cranberry Rail Trail, is named for the Cranberry, Cherry, and Gauley Rivers it travels along or across. The route begins in downtown Richwood, immediately behind the visitor center, which is housed in the old passenger and freight railway depot.

For the first 6 miles of the trail, you travel through towns and adjacent to private property, with the 3 miles between Richwood and Fenwick being the toughest. The route here parallels the beautiful Cherry River; it is well worth the trip for the view. Shortly after the trail crosses WV 55 in Holcomb, it enters Monongahela National Forest. Here, the route—now a more dedicated trail—becomes much easier to follow, with no road crossings or private property abutting it and only the roar of the

Historic relics dot this 16-mile trail.

County
Nicholas

Endpoints
Behind the depot near Oakford Ave. (Richwood) to Gauley River near Powder House Road or Bishop Ln. (Craigsville)

Mileage
16

Type
Rail-Trail

Roughness Index
3

Surface
Dirt, Gravel

rushing water to keep you company. A beautiful waterfall on the right is visible from the conveniently located viewing platform.

After you cross the Cranberry River, the path takes you through the curving, 640-foot Sarah's Tunnel, which is pitch-dark at its center. One mile beyond the tunnel, you arrive at the trail's end. There are plans to extend the trail another 10 miles into the forest, but until that happens, please adhere to the no-trespassing signs.

For a longer visit, cabins are located next to the trail after you enter Monongahela National Forest. Despite the breathtaking beauty of the Cranberry Tri-Rivers Rail Trail, the surface can be difficult due to the protruding tree roots and rocks; be prepared for thick, sticky mud just after the winter thaw.

CONTACT: wvrtc.org

DIRECTIONS

To reach the Richwood trailhead from I-64, take Exit 156. Follow US 60 W for 10.2 miles. Turn right onto Main St., and follow it 18.7 miles. Turn right onto Main St./Nettie-Fenwick Road, and travel 8.4 miles. After crossing Cherry River, turn right onto WV 39, and go 3.1 miles to Oakford Ave. The trail is the gravel/dirt path behind the old railway depot, now a visitor center.

The Holcomb trailhead is the recommended starting point for the trip through Monongahela National Forest. To reach it, follow the directions to the Richwood trailhead up to the crossing of Cherry River. Once you cross the river, take a left onto WV 55, and go 2.3 miles. From the Richwood trailhead, this access point is 5.4 miles north on WV 55. The trail crosses WV 55 on the east side of the Cherry River (if you are coming from Richwood, look for the trail before the bridge over the river). You can park at the trail entrance on the north side of the road.

44 Glade Creek Trail

Situated in the heart of West Virginia's pristine New River Gorge National River, the Glade Creek Trail has something for everyone. Once a narrow-gage railroad corridor that hauled coal from remote mines within New River Gorge, Glade Creek Trail is now a great destination for hiking. You can also swim, fish, camp, and kayak.

Start your trip at the trailhead located near the confluence of Glade Creek and the New River. Here, you will find several well-maintained campsites, picnic tables, and restrooms. The trailhead is also home to a popular swimming hole, a great place to cool off after a hot summer hike. Once on the trail, take in the beautiful scenery and picturesque waterfalls provided by Glade Creek as it rushes past on its way to the New River. Be sure to bring your fishing pole; the lower section of Glade Creek is an official catch-and-release trout stream. As you follow the meandering

County
Raleigh

Endpoints
Glade Creek Road (Prince, New River Gorge National River) to Scott Branch Road/CR 22 (Crow)

Mileage
5.8

Type
Rail-Trail

Roughness Index
3

Surface
Dirt, Gravel

Fishermen and kayakers will be eyeing the rushing waters of Glade Creek.

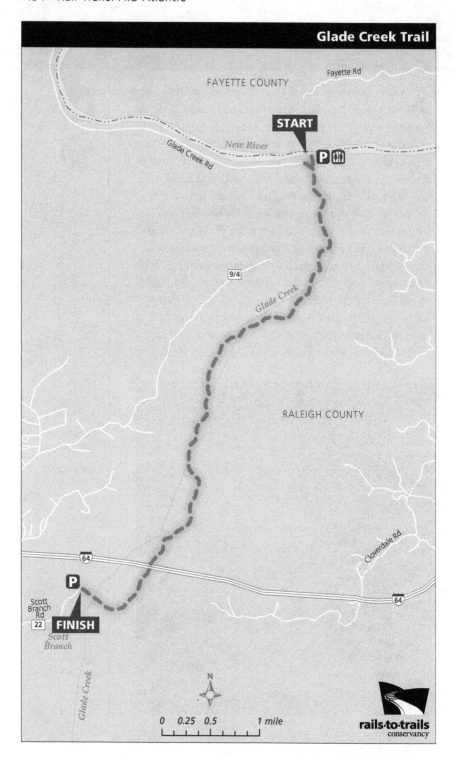

path along the banks of the creek, keep an eye out for native wildlife and the occasional adventurous kayaker attempting to navigate the creek's swift rapids.

The Glade Creek Trail has a moderate grade, but the first half can be difficult to hike because the path is slightly narrow and strewn with large rocks and tree branches. Once you cross the trail's lone bridge, near the 3-mile mark, the path becomes wider and better maintained. If you're looking for a challenge, hit the more strenuous Kates Falls Trail located about 1 mile before the end of Glade Creek Trail.

CONTACT: nps.gov/neri/planyourvisit/glade-creek-trails.htm

DIRECTIONS

To reach the northern trailhead at Glade Creek from I-64, take Exit 124/Beckley. Go north on Joe L. Smith Dr. for 0.7 mile, and turn left onto Brookshire Ln. Make an immediate right onto US 19, and follow it 1.8 miles north. Turn right onto WV 41, and travel 4.8 miles. Then turn right to remain on WV 41, and follow it 3.9 miles toward Prince. Turn right onto Glade Creek Road, just before the bridge in Prince. Follow the gravel road for 5.6 miles to the Glade Creek Trailhead.

To reach the southern trailhead, where Pinch Creek meets Glade Creek, from I-64, take Exit 129A, and follow WV 9 S for 0.5 mile. Turn left onto CR 22/Scott Branch Road, and proceed approximately 1.25 miles to a parking area along Glade Creek (you'll cross a bridge). Note: High-clearance, four-wheel-drive vehicles are recommended, as CR 22 is steep, rocky, and often muddy.

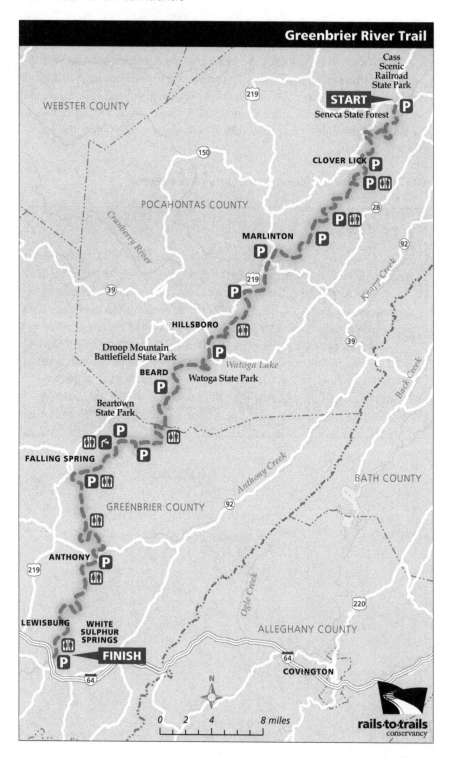

Greenbrier River Trail

Cass Scenic Railroad State Park

START

Seneca State Forest

WEBSTER COUNTY

219

150

POCAHONTAS COUNTY

Cranberry River

CLOVER LICK

28

92

MARLINTON

39

219

HILLSBORO

Knapp Creek

Droop Mountain Battlefield State Park

Watoga Lake

Watoga State Park

39

Back Creek

BEARD

Beartown State Park

FALLING SPRING

GREENBRIER COUNTY

Anthony Creek

92

BATH COUNTY

ANTHONY

219

Ogle Creek

220

LEWISBURG

WHITE SULPHUR SPRINGS

FINISH

ALLEGHANY COUNTY

64

COVINGTON

64

N

0   2   4   8 miles

rails·to·trails
conservancy

45 Greenbrier River Trail

West Virginia's beautiful Greenbrier River Trail is one of America's premier rail-trails, well-liked by bicyclists, hikers, walkers, and cross-country skiers. Most of the trail runs along the gorgeous Greenbrier River and passes through picturesque countryside as it winds through the river valley. There is no doubt you will see many species of interesting wildlife along this wonderful route.

Today, the trail is operated and maintained by West Virginia State Parks, but it was originally built for use by one of the many West Virginia railroads that supplied the once-prospering local timber industry. Now the corridor is for recreational use, with campsites and many restroom and water facilities scattered along its route. The trail hosts the annual Great Greenbrier River Race, which includes canoeing, biking, and running.

Counties
Greenbrier, Pocahontas

Endpoints
Stonehouse Road near I-64 (North Caldwell) to Deer Creek Road at WV 66/Back Mountain Road (Cass Scenic Railroad State Park in Cass)

Mileage
77

Type
Rail-Trail

Roughness Index
1

Surface
Gravel

The Greenbrier River accompanies the trail as it swoops through the valley.

Even though the mileposts start at the southern end of the Greenbrier River Trail, it's best to start your trip on the slightly uphill grade at the northern end at Cass Scenic Railroad State Park and follow the river downstream. The first town you will pass is Clover Lick, a lovely little Appalachian town with rustic remnants of the old railroad depot that once served the booming logging industry.

Beyond the Clover Lick trailhead, the trail proceeds south, winding 20 miles downstream through some of the most scenic and remote wilderness landscapes in West Virginia. This section ends at the only large town you will encounter along the trail—Marlinton, which features some great lunch spots and bed-and-breakfasts. You can find a trailside information center in Marlinton's old train station near mile 55. As you proceed south from Marlinton, you will cross the river twice before reaching the halfway point at Beard.

One of the great things about the Greenbrier River Trail is the opportunity to see remnants of the old railroad, including many whistle posts and historical mile markers. Beyond Beard (milepost 31) is one of the trail's two spectacular tunnels: the 402-foot-long Droop Mountain Tunnel, built in 1900, and Sharps Tunnel, 511 feet long and built in 1899. Continuing south, beyond Anthony (at mile 15), the trail crosses two old railroad bridges and eventually reaches its southern terminus at North Caldwell (milepost 3). This trailhead is located just outside Lewisburg, which has a variety of shops, restaurants, and lodging.

CONTACT: greenbrierrivertrail.com

DIRECTIONS

To reach the northern trailhead at Cass, take I-64 to Exit 169/Lewisburg. Follow US 219 60.4 miles north to WV 66 E. Turn right onto WV 66/Back Mountain Road, and go 2.3 miles. The trailhead will be on your right, just off Deer Creek Road. Or take WV 28 to WV 66 W, and look for the trailhead just off WV 66 on your left after 5.2 miles.

To reach the southern trailhead at North Caldwell, take I-64 E to Exit 175/US 60. Turn left (west) onto US 60, and go 2.7 miles to CR 38/Stonehouse Road. The trailhead will be on your right in 1.4 miles. If you're coming from I-64 W, take Exit 169 to US 219; travel north 0.5 mile to CR 30/Brush Road, and turn right. From here, drive another 0.5 mile to CR 38/Stonehouse Road. The trailhead will be on the left in 3 miles.

46 Green Mountain Trail

The scenic Green Mountain Trail provides foot access to some of the most remote areas of Otter Creek Wilderness in the Monongahela National Forest. Stretching 4 miles, this trail offers stunning views of the remote West Virginia backcountry and has less traffic than other trails in the region because of its difficult accessibility. The Green Mountain Trail is great for either an overnight backpacking trip or a long and challenging day hike.

Though the trail itself is 4.1 miles long, there is some considerable hiking to get to the actual trailhead. You'll have to hike in from the Big Springs Gap trailhead or either of the Otter Creek trailheads, which are located at Congdon Run (Forest Road 303 in Dry Fork) and Dry Fork Road (where the Dry Fork tributary meets Otter Creek, in Parsons).

County
Tucker

Endpoints
Near FR 701 in Monongahela National Forest (near Parsons)

Mileage
4.1

Type
Rail-Trail

Roughness Index
3

Surface
Dirt

Some of West Virginia's most remote wilderness is waiting for you on this trail.

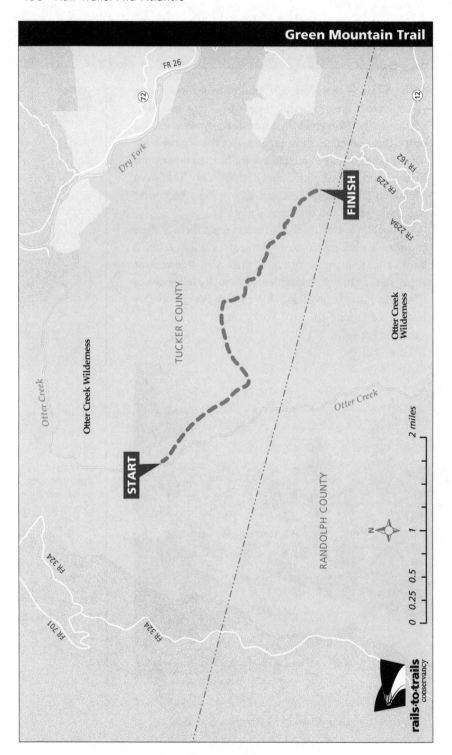

The Green Mountain Trail at first climbs steeply out of the Otter Creek valley and provides breathtaking views of the surrounding area. It levels out after about 2 miles and follows a high mountain plateau before reaching the junction with the Possession Camp Trail in 2.7 miles. The trail concludes with a 1.3-mile ascent through thickly wooded brush at the top of Green Mountain. The end of the route is marked by a cairn indicating the start of the Shavers Mountain Trail.

CONTACT: www.fs.usda.gov/mnf

DIRECTIONS

To reach Big Springs Gap trailhead from Parsons, take First St. north to Billings Ave., and turn right onto Billings. Billings turns into CR 219. After 2.4 miles, turn right onto FR 701. After another 2.8 miles, take a slight left to remain on FR 701, and follow the signs to the trailhead, which will be on the left after another 0.6 mile.

Green Mountain Trail travels through the Otter Creek Wilderness.

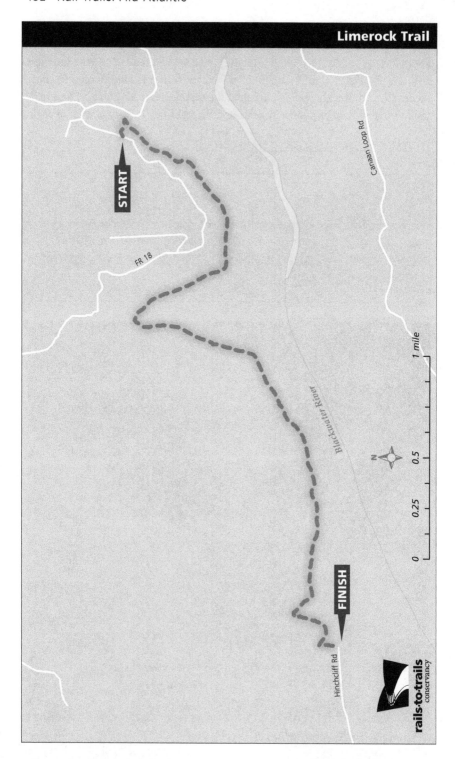

The Limerock Trail is pure West Virginia: From Forest Road 18, the 4-mile rail-trail passes through rhododendron forests and alongside rocky cliffs and rushing streams. You begin with the roar of the rapids from Tub Run, and the sounds quietly disappear as you head west down the ridge toward Hendricks.

You will have to traverse a stream several places along the trail. When the water level is low, it's possible to do this by rock-hopping; otherwise, your feet will get wet. After about 1.5 miles, you will reach Big Run, where the blue blazes marking the path become more sporadic; however, the trail is still easy to follow. After Big Run, you will come to Flat Rock Run. Departing briefly from the trail and following this creek downhill will bring you to a 20-foot waterfall.

County
Tucker

Endpoints
FR 18 (Hambleton) to Blackwater Canyon Trail (Monongahela National Forest in Hendricks)

Mileage
4

Type
Rail-Trail

Roughness Index
2

Surface
Dirt

The blue blazes become more sporadic after the first 1.5 miles of this trail; keep your eyes peeled.

The trail ends at the Blackwater Canyon Trail. To avoid the Limerock Trail's uphill return hike, you can follow the Blackwater Canyon about 6 miles north to Coketon or 2 miles south to Hendricks.

CONTACT: www.fs.usda.gov/mnf

DIRECTIONS

From Elkins, take US 219 N toward Parsons, following the signs to remain on US 219. About 7 miles after you pass Parsons, you will see a sign on the right for FR 18. Turn right here and then take the next left, which is actually a continuation of FR 18 (no sign indicates this). You will need a four-wheel-drive vehicle to reach the trail on this road, as the road is not paved and is very rutted, with at least one stream crossing. After about 3.5 miles, you will see a sign for the Limerock Trail on your right. You may park on the side of the road.

For a longer hike, you can take US 219 toward Parsons and then take WV 72 south 3.1 miles to Hendricks. On your right, you will see the Allegheny Highlands Trailhead. Park in this lot, located near the Blackwater River on your right. Take the Allegheny Highlands Trail across WV 72 to the Blackwater Canyon Trail. This trail will meet Limerock about 2 miles north of Hendricks.

48 Mon River Rail-Trail System

The Mon River Rail-Trail System spans a total of 48.7 miles through three counties—Marion, Monongalia, and Preston—with Morgantown, West Virginia, serving as a central hub for the network. Morgantown is known as the home of West Virginia University, the inspiration for a Joni Mitchell song ("Morning Morgantown"), and the birthplace of actor Don Knotts.

Three of the trails hug the Monongahela River, one of a few American rivers that flow north. The Mon eventually arrives in Pittsburgh, where it joins the Allegheny River to form the Ohio River.

This system of trails, which follows a former CSX rail line, comprises four segments, each with its own name and unique amenities.

CONTACT: montrails.org

Caperton Trail

The central point of the Caperton Trail is located in Morgantown at the heart of the Mon River Rail-Trail system, and the route goes north to Star City and south to White Park in the First Ward neighborhood. The paved rail-trail, named after a former West Virginia governor, parallels the Monongahela River and travels past retail businesses, West Virginia University, and industrial areas, as well as the back decks of eateries that cater to trail users.

Heading north out of Morgantown, the route passes through several downtown parks, including Hazel Ruby McQuain Park, West Virginia University's Core Arboretum, and the Edith B. Barill Riverfront Park in Star City. Hazel Ruby McQuain Park is also the western endpoint of the Deckers Creek Trail, which heads 19 miles southeast to Reedsville.

At the Caperton Trail's northern end in Star City, continue along the river via the connecting Mon River Trail North to the Pennsylvania state line; south of Morgantown,

County
Monongalia

Endpoints
Mon River Trail North at Edith B. Barill Riverfront Park (Star City) to Mon River Trail South near White Park (Morgantown)

Mileage
6

Type
Rail-Trail

Roughness Index
1

Surface
Asphalt

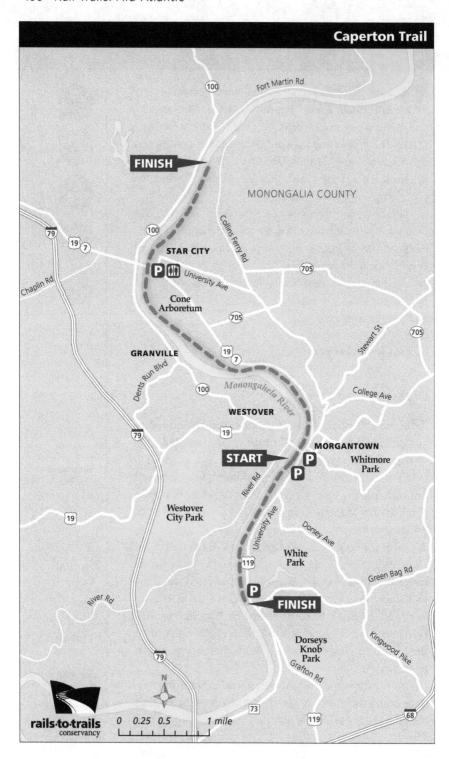

Caperton Trail

the Caperton Trail links to the Mon River Trail South to access Marion County and Prickett's Fort State Park. All three trails follow the same former CSX rail line.

DIRECTIONS

Park at Hazel Ruby McQuain Park in Morgantown. From I-68, take Exit 7 and turn right onto CR 857 south; go 1 mile. Turn left onto US 119/Mileground Road/N. Willey St. Go 3.2 miles, and then turn left as US 119 becomes High St. Go 0.3 mile, and turn right onto Moreland St. Hazel Ruby McQuain Park is in less than 0.25 mile.

In Star City, parking is available at Edith B. Barill Riverfront Park. Take WV 7 N (Don Knotts Blvd./University Ave./Beechhurst Ave./Monongahela Blvd.) about 2.7 miles from downtown Morgantown to Star City. Turn right onto Boyers Ave., and then take an immediate left onto Leeway St. In 0.1 mile, take the access road beside 84 Lumber to reach the parking lot. (From I-68, follow the directions to Hazel Ruby McQuain Park above, but pass High St., and then turn right onto WV 7/US 19 to Star City.)

A mural along the Caperton Trail

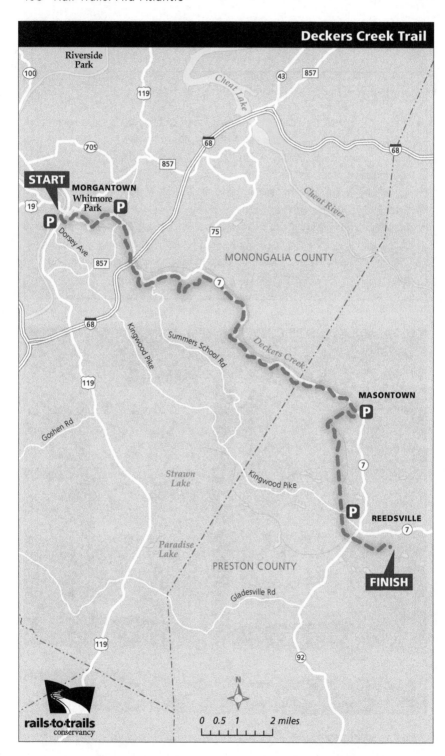

Deckers Creek Trail

Deckers Creek Trail is the gem of the system. Beginning at the confluence of the Monongahela River and Deckers Creek at Hazel Ruby McQuain Park, the trail stretches 19 miles to the southeast, gaining 1,000 feet as it climbs out of the Monongahela River valley. It parallels Deckers Creek and WV Scenic Byway 7 on its way to Reedsville, West Virginia, in Preston County. But the most memorable feature of this landscape is Deckers Creek itself.

Because of the steady grade, the trail passes a series of dramatic rapids and waterfalls, while the creek noisily rushes headlong toward the Monongahela. Highly experienced kayakers paddle Deckers Creek, which has some Class VI rapids, and rock climbing is also popular in the region.

The first 2.5 miles of Deckers Creek Trail are paved and pass through an unremarkable urban landscape in Morgantown. The route provides easy access to Marilla Park, which has a swimming pool and water slides, tennis courts, and a playground, as well as neighboring restaurants and food stores. After passing under I-68, the surface changes to crushed stone. As the ascent begins, you enter a rural

Counties
Monongalia, Preston

Endpoints
Hazel Ruby McQuain Park (Morgantown) to Morgan Mine Road (Reedsville)

Mileage
19

Type
Rail-Trail

Roughness Index
2

Surface
Asphalt, Crushed Stone

A short scramble rewards trail users with incredible views of Deckers Creek.

landscape distinguished by hemlocks, rhododendrons, and a smattering of residences. The trail provides a close-up view of Greer Limestone, an active quarry business. Near the communities of Masontown and Bretz, the path passes an abandoned row of coke ovens, remnants from a large coal-mining industry that are now a National Historic Landmark.

As the route approaches its endpoint near Reedsville, the grade flattens and the woods give way to wetland areas that feature cattails and red-winged blackbirds. Less than 1 mile away on WV 92 is the Arthurdale New Deal Homestead Museum. The entire community of Arthurdale is on the National Register of Historic Places, recognized as the nation's first New Deal Homestead Community.

For those not accustomed to hard pedaling, you can start on the Reedsville end and enjoy a pleasant ride downhill into Morgantown. At the start in Hazel Ruby McQuain Park, you can also pick up the Caperton section of the Mon River Rail-Trail system.

DIRECTIONS

Park in Morgantown at Hazel Ruby McQuain Park or in Saberton at Marilla Park. Masontown and Reedsville also have trailheads with parking.

To reach Hazel Ruby McQuain Park from I-68, take Exit 7 and turn right onto CR 857 south; go 1 mile. Turn left onto US 119/Mileground Road/N. Willey St. Go 3.2 miles, and turn left as US 119 becomes High St. Go 0.3 mile, and turn right onto Moreland St. Hazel Ruby McQuain Park is in less than 0.25 mile.

To reach the Masontown trailhead from Morgantown, take WV 7 E for 10.4 miles. Make a sharp right onto Bridgeway Ave., and take the first right onto Sand Bank Road. The trailhead will be on the right. From Reedsville, take WV 7 W for 3 miles. Turn left onto Depot Way; after 0.3 mile, turn left onto Sand Bank Road. The trailhead is to the right.

To reach the Reedsville trailhead from Morgantown, take WV 7 southeast toward Reedsville. After 0.7 mile, take a sharp left onto Rogers Ave. to remain on WV 7. In another 0.7 mile, continue straight to stay on WV 7. Follow it for another 14.4 miles. In Reedsville, continue straight on WV 92. Go 0.4 mile to the trailhead.

To reach the access point in Marilla Park, take WV 7 southeast for 0.7 mile, and continue straight on E. Brockway Ave. for 0.7 mile to a parking lot. A bridge crosses Deckers Creek to reach the trail.

Mon River Trail North

The Mon River Trail North has a crushed stone surface and begins in Star City where the Caperton section ends. The trail courses northward, quickly entering dense woodlands at the edge of the Monongahela River and following the waterway for approximately 6 miles to the Pennsylvania state line, where it abruptly ends.

Trail users can continue south from Star City on the Caperton Trail to reach downtown Morgantown and other trails in the system, including the Mon River Trail South and Deckers Creek Trail.

DIRECTIONS

Parking is available at Edith B. Barill Riverfront Park. From downtown Morgantown, take WV 7 N (Don Knotts Blvd./University Ave./Beechhurst Ave./Monongahela Blvd.) about 3 miles to Star City. Turn right (north) onto Boyers Ave., and then take an immediate left onto Leeway St. In 0.1 mile, take the access road beside 84 Lumber to reach the parking lot.

County
Monongalia

Endpoints
Pennsylvania state line at Fifth Ave. (Port Marion, PA) to Caperton Trail at Edith B. Barrill Riverfront Park (Star City, WV)

Mileage
6

Type
Rail-Trail

Roughness Index
1

Surface
Crushed Stone

The Monongahela River is a key feature in the Mon River Rail-Trail System.

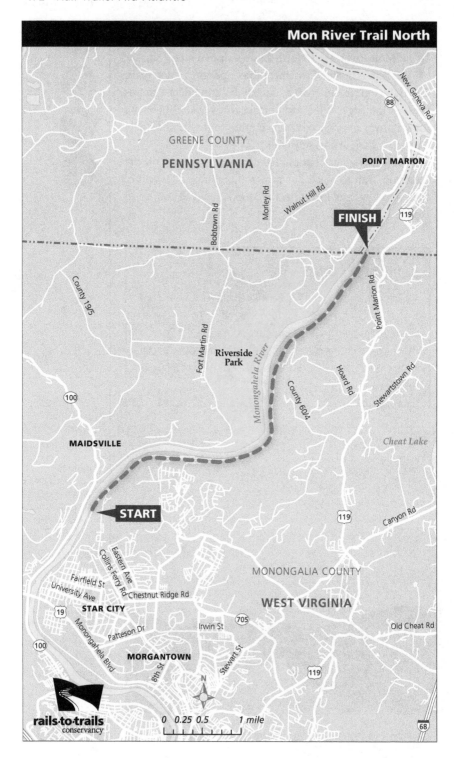

Mon River Trail North

Mon River Trail South

The Mon River Trail South begins where the paved trail becomes crushed stone at the southern edge of Morgantown (also the southern end of the Caperton section). From there, it meanders for 17.7 miles to Prickett's Fort State Park. The Mon South lazily winds through a wooded river valley with many scenic river views, occasional waterfalls, and a variety of wildflowers in the spring and autumn. At the southern end at Prickett's Fort, pick up the Marion County (MC) Trail.

DIRECTIONS

Park at the Uffington boat dock, off of CR 73, where I-79 crosses the river. From downtown Morgantown, take US 119 2.1 miles south. Take a slight right onto CR 73/Smithtown Road, and follow it for 1.6 miles. Before reaching I-79, turn right onto Round Bottom Road, where you will find a parking lot for the trailhead straight ahead.

Parking is also available at the southern end at Prickett's Fort. To reach Prickett's Fort State Park from I-79, take Exit 139 north of Fairmont and follow signs to the park. At the exit, turn right onto Bunner Ridge Road, and follow it 0.4 mile. Take a left onto Meadowdale Road, and then take an immediate right onto Prickett's Fort Road. Follow it 2.3 miles, continuing straight as it turns into Overfort Ln., and park at the lot. A short jaunt along the Marion County (MC) Trail will take you to the Mon River Trail South.

Counties
Marion, Monongalia

Endpoints
White Park (Morgantown city limits) to Prickett's Fort State Park (Fairmont)

Mileage
17.7

Type
Rail-Trail

Roughness Index
1

Surface
Crushed Stone

Along the Mon River, enjoy views of a series of locks and dams that support navigation on the waterway.

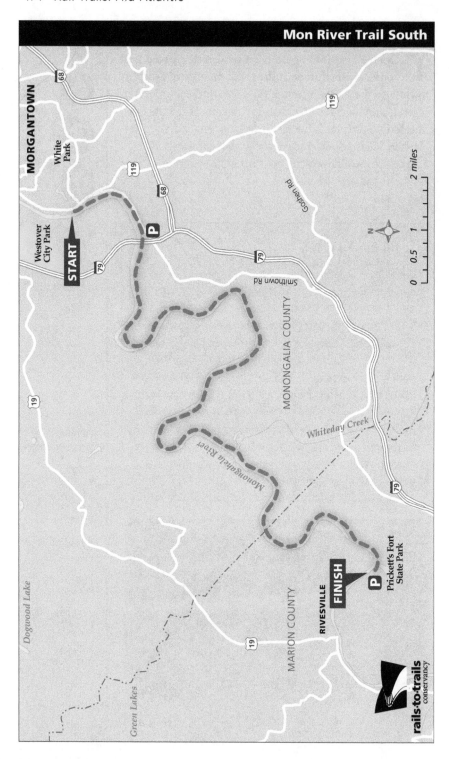

First and foremost, the North Bend Trail is a beautiful trail with splendid railroad elements and welcoming trail towns. However, it is best enjoyed by foot. Despite its potential as a multiuse path, the upkeep on the trail makes bicycling difficult to impossible. So for a happier time for all, consider hoofing it (whether on your own two feet or a horse's four).

The trail is part of the 5,500-mile, coast-to-coast American Discovery Trail. Stretching nearly 72 miles from I-77 near Parkersburg (Cedar Grove) to Wolf Summit, the route travels through an impressive 13 tunnels (10 passable), crosses 36 bridges, and passes through or near an assortment of state, county, and local parks.

Though it is easily accessible from I-77 and I-79 and runs parallel to US 50, the trail passes through wild and natural areas. You will find an abundance of wildlife,

Counties
Doddridge, Harrison, Ritchie, Wood

Endpoints
Happy Valley Road/ CR 47/26 (Cedar Grove) to School St./Old US 50 (Wolf Summit)

Mileage
72

Type
Rail-Trail

Roughness Index
3

Surface
Ballast, Cinder, Crushed Stone, Dirt, Grass, Gravel

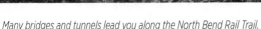

Many bridges and tunnels lead you along the North Bend Rail Trail.

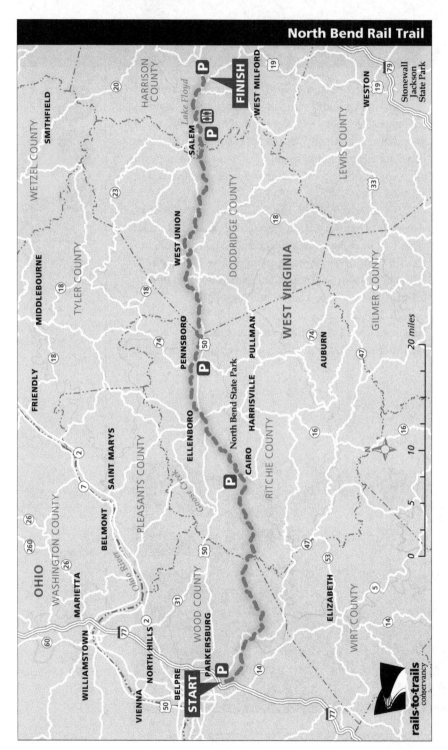

including deer and beavers, and the farmlands surrounding the small, rural communities along the railroad corridor provide prime bird-watching. The North Bend Rail Trail's many points of interest include a former stagecoach inn in Pennsboro, a marble factory, hand-blown glass factories, outlet stores, arts-and-crafts markets, fairs and festivals, veteran memorials, and a bike shop/ general store. Its history highlights sites of train robberies and the legend of the ghost of tunnel 19, the Silver Run Tunnel.

The Baltimore & Ohio Railroad constructed the rail corridor between 1853 and 1857, in the tumultuous years before the Civil War and the creation of the state of West Virginia. Thirteen of the railroad's original tunnels remain. The number 10 tunnel, west of Ellenboro, is 337 feet long and is a raw, or natural, tunnel, meaning it was bored through solid rock. Many of the tunnels are quite long and require a flashlight or headlamp to safely navigate them.

The true gem of this trail is the stunning natural scenery. Beyond the spectacular bridges and tunnels, the undisturbed beauty makes you feel more like the explorers Lewis and Clark than a 21st-century hiker. And like those same adventurers, you're apt to have some wildlife encounters as well. Black bears, bountiful deer, grouse, and more may cross your path.

You'll also encounter other trail users, particularly near the many quaint towns along the route that have wholly embraced the rail-trail, building eateries that will satisfy even the hungriest of hikers. Towns, such as Cairo, Pennsboro, and Salem, have all had restaurants pop up next to the trail. The locals are happy to share a story of the old rail line, and the staff welcome even the sweatiest of customers.

CONTACT: wvparks.com/northbendrailtrail

DIRECTIONS

To reach the Parkersburg trailhead, take I-77 to Exit 174/Staunton Ave., and turn east onto WV 47/Staunton Ave. Take the first right turn (about 0.2 mile from the interstate) onto Old WV 47/Cedar Grove Road. Continue about 0.7 mile, and turn right onto Happy Valley Road. Travel approximately 0.4 mile until you see a large house on the left. Immediately after the stone wall (Millers Landing) is the North Bend Rail Trail. Park on the gravel section opposite the trailhead.

To begin at Wolf Summit, take US 50 E to Wolf Summit (about 65 miles from Parkersburg). About 6.5 miles after passing Salem International University, take the Wolf Summit exit, and turn left onto Sycamore Road. Immediately turn right onto Old US 50, and go 0.3 mile, where the road meets School St. The trailhead is on the left.

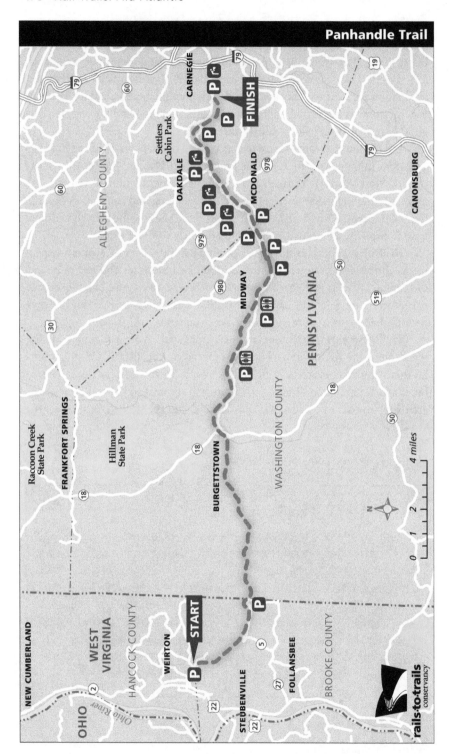

The Panhandle Trail is another jewel in the Pittsburgh metro area trail system. A Conrail line known as the Panhandle Railroad once connected Pittsburgh to Cincinnati, Chicago, and St. Louis on this route. The rail corridor has been transformed into a multiuse, nonmotorized trail stretching nearly 29 miles, from Weirton, West Virginia, to Carnegie, Pennsylvania.

Today, the wide trail is open to pedestrians and cyclists, with many easy access points along the way. Beginning in West Virginia, the start of the trail is actually some 3,000 feet to the east; it's a dead-end, and trail users won't miss much if they simply begin at the trailhead off Colliers Road. The trail follows the route of Harmon Creek—which feeds into the Ohio River—for the entirety of its West Virginia segment, as well as several miles through Pennsylvania. (In Midway, Pennsylvania, it picks up alongside Robinson Run and stays with that creek for the remainder of the trail.) At the confluence of Harmon Creek and Paris Run, the trail crosses the West Virginia–Pennsylvania state line, marked with a white rail sign.

Counties
Allegheny (PA), Brooke, Washington (PA)

Endpoints
Police Lodge Road at US 22 (Weirton, WV) to Walkers Mill Road/ PA 3028 (Carnegie, PA)

Mileage
29

Type
Rail-Trail

Roughness Index
2

Surface
Crushed Stone

This gorgeous trail connects directly to the strong networks of trails in Western Pennsylvania.

With such a close relationship to rivers and creeks, the route features many small bridge crossings as it cuts through the rolling and, by turns, rocky hillside, showcasing many opportunities for photos, especially in the fall. Spring and summer, when flowering shrubs and wildflowers dress up various landscaped trailheads and access points, are great times to bike the Panhandle. June–October, the Collier Friends of the Panhandle Trail sponsors several annual events here. The trail passes through several small towns, such as Burgettstown, Pennsylvania, where you can grab a bite to eat or quench your thirst at near-trailside stores or restaurants. This is a region familiar with trail users, particularly when you approach McDonald. Just north of the Noblestown Road crossing, the Panhandle Trail veers to the north to intersect with the Montour Trail between the village of Primrose and the town of McDonald; ultimately, the Montour Trail links to Washington, D.C., via the Great Allegheny Passage and C&O Canal Towpath. Continue east to finish out the Panhandle Trail where it merges into Walkers Mill Road outside of Carnegie.

Recognized as a valuable resource and landmark for residents, the Panhandle Trail was the 100th successful rail-trail project in Pennsylvania. As such, it generally enjoys speedy and routine maintenance from the many state government organizations that oversee it, though the Friends group maintains the 2.6-mile section from Walkers Mill to Greg Station.

CONTACT: **panhandletrail.org**

DIRECTIONS

To reach the Weirton, WV, trailhead from Pittsburgh, take I-376 W to Exit 60A. Follow US 22 W for 22.6 miles, and take Exit 3. Turn left onto Harmon Creek Road, heading south. After 0.2 mile, turn right onto Colliers Road, and then make another right to stay on Colliers. Trailhead parking is on the right in a lot under US 22.

To reach the Carnegie trailhead, take I-79 to Exit 57. Turn right (west) on W. Main St., which turns into Noblestown Road. Continue 1.7 miles to Walkers Mill Road, and turn left. Go 0.1 mile to a parking lot on the right, where the trailhead is marked.

To reach the Montour and Panhandle trailhead near McDonald, PA, take I-376 to Exit 60A. Follow US 22 W for 1.4 miles, and take the exit to Hankey Farms. Turn left (south) onto Oakdale Road, and follow it for 1.5 miles. Turn right onto PA 978 N, and follow it for 0.5 mile. Continue straight on N. Branch Road for 4 miles. Turn left onto PA 980; after 1.9 miles, turn right to Noblestown Road. The trailhead parking and access is at the intersection of Johns Ave. and Noblestown Road, about 1 mile farther.

51 Potts Valley Rail Trail

The Potts Valley Rail Trail is built on a former corridor of the Norfolk & Western rail line. Called the Potts Valley Branch, it operated between 1909 and 1932 and was built to haul iron ore, and then timber, out of the lush mountain region. Much of the 5-mile rail-trail lies within Jefferson National Forest, while a small portion is on a private property right-of-way. Along the trail, you will find interpretive signs about Potts Valley's history, as well as benches where you can stop and take in the scenery or the quiet solitude of the forest.

The southwest trailhead lies a few hundred yards from the Eastern Continental Divide, which at that location separates the headwaters of Stony Creek (a New River tributary) and Potts Creek (a James River tributary). Mountain ridges on each side of the valley trail reach elevations of between 3,700 and 4,100 feet, and the trail overlooks

Take in the scenery and solitude along the Potts Valley Rail Trail.

County
Monroe

Endpoints
WV Secondary 17/
Waiteville Road (Monroe
County border) to WV
Secondary 15/5/Rays
Siding Road (Waiteville)

Mileage
4.5

Type
Rail-Trail

Roughness Index
2

Surface
Dirt, Grass

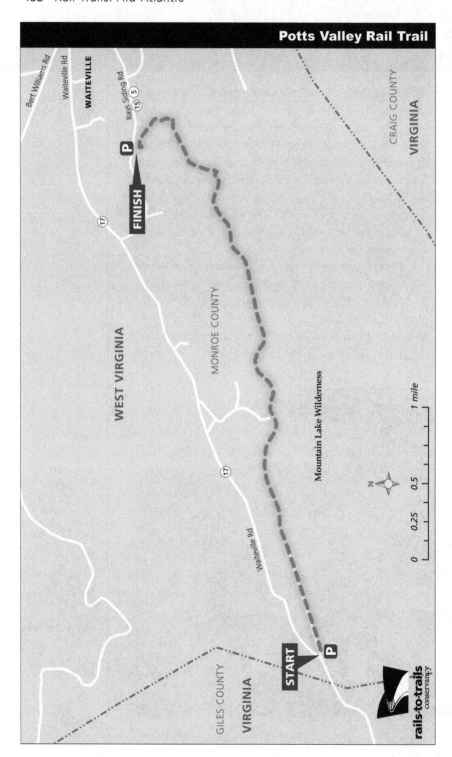

the South Fork of Potts Creek, a brook trout stream. The route begins in West Virginia, just shy of the border with Virginia, on WV Secondary 17/Waiteville Road. The trail travels through a forest of mixed pines and hardwoods, with rhododendrons in the understory. Because the path was once a railroad track, the slopes along the Potts Valley Rail Trail are gentle. Beginning at the southwest trailhead, you will follow the border of the Mountain Lake Wilderness, the largest wilderness area in the Jefferson National Forest.

Take one of the side trails and view the handiwork of stone masons, who carved culverts for the forest's ubiquitous streams to run underneath the rail line. At about the 3-mile point, you arrive at the site of the former Crosier trestle. The wooden bridge, once 98 feet tall and 600 feet long, carried trains across the stream. Unfortunately, rebuilding it for foot traffic was not feasible, so the rail-trail detours here, downslope away from the railbed. Notice the hand-cut stone pillars that once supported the railroad bridge.

About 0.75 mile beyond Crosier Branch (a stream you must cross), the trail enters private property and continues for another 0.5 mile to the northwest trailhead. A bench just before the endpoint provides a great location for enjoying the pastoral scenery. The trail ends about a mile or so above Waiteville, but if you continue (following public roads), you come across the old Waiteville depot and then The Depot Lodge in Paint Bank, another former depot that is now a lodge. In the nearby brick building, you'll find a general store and restaurant. Mountain bikers can do a loop ride by using WV Secondary 15/5/Rays Siding Road and WV Secondary 17/Waiteville Road to return to the Potts Valley Rail Trailhead.

CONTACT: travelmonroe.com/adventure.html

DIRECTIONS

From US 219 in Union, WV: Follow WV 3 E for 9 miles to Gap Mills, and turn right onto Zenith Road. After 3.5 miles, turn left onto Limestone Hill Road/Gap Mills Road. Follow it for 5.5 miles across Peter's Mountain. At the bottom of the mountain, turn right onto WV Secondary 17/Waiteville Road. Follow WV Secondary 17 for 1 mile to Waiteville, and then for another 4.5 miles to the southwest trailhead, on the left, not far from the Virginia state line.

From US 460: Take US 460 about 4 miles east of Pearisburg, VA, and turn left onto VA 635. After 5.5 miles, turn left to stay on VA 635. Continue for another 12 miles. At the Monroe County line, VA 635 becomes WV Secondary 17. The southwest trailhead will be on the right, roughly 0.25 mile in from the border.

From VA 311 in Paint Bank, VA: Follow VA 600 (WV Secondary 17 at the Monroe County line) for 12 miles to Waiteville. Continue on WV Secondary 17/Waiteville Road for another 4.5 miles to the southwest trailhead, on your right.

Northeast trailhead from the southwest trailhead: Follow WV Secondary 17/Waiteville Road to the northeast for 3.3 miles. Turn right onto WV Secondary 15/5/Rays Siding Road. Follow it for 0.75 mile to the trailhead, on the right.

Northeast trailhead from Waiteville: Follow WV Secondary 17/Waiteville Road to the southwest for 1.5 miles. Turn left onto WV Secondary 15/5/Rays Siding Road. Follow it for 0.75 mile to the trailhead on the right.

With breathtaking scenery, numerous bridges, and several impressive overlooks, it is no wonder that the wide, well-maintained Rend Trail (formerly known as the Thurmond–Minden Trail) is one of the most popular trails in the New River Gorge National River area. The route traces the Arbuckle Branch railroad corridor along the banks of three rushing waterways from the old mining community of Minden to the old railroad town of Thurmond. Though the Arbuckle Branch, built in 1906, became inactive long ago, you can still see evidence of coal mining along this route.

The trail begins along scenic Arbuckle Creek and follows the raging water of this tributary to its confluence with the New River. Near the banks of the New River, be sure to stop at the overlook for an incredible view, which includes that of an active railroad line. After a brief journey

Numerous bridges offer scenic river views along the trail.

County
Fayette

Endpoints
CR 25/Thurmond Road
(Oak Hill) to Minden Ave.
(Minden)

Mileage
3.2

Type
Rail-Trail

Roughness Index
2

Surface
Dirt, Gravel

along the New River, the path heads south along the quiet banks of Dunloup Creek. The trail ends at a parking lot near a great fishing hole.

While the Rend Trail provides an excellent path for bicycling and hiking, bikers beware: A set of stairs built around the remains of a rockslide can hinder your journey if you are unable to carry your bike up and down the wooden steps.

Note: A portion of the Rend Trail (the second bridge from the Minden side, which is 1.27 miles in from the Minden trailhead and 1.96 miles in from the Thurmond trailhead) is closed due to structural damage and may be closed for several years. Check the website below for updates.

CONTACT: nps.gov/neri/planyourvisit/thurmondminden_trail.htm

DIRECTIONS

To access the Thurmond trailhead, head north from Beckley on US 19 for approximately 11 miles. Take the Glen Jean–Thurmond exit, and turn left onto WV 16/WV 61. After 0.4 mile, turn right onto Glen Jean Ln., and then make an immediate left onto McKell Ave. Turn left onto Thurmond Road/WV 25. Follow the signs for the Rend Trail or Thurmond–Minden Trail, located 5 miles outside of Glen Jean off WV 25 on the left.

To reach the Minden trailhead from Beckley, head north approximately 15 miles on US 19. Take the Oak Hill/Main St. exit, and turn right onto E. Main St. at the end of the ramp. Turn left at Minden Road, and follow it for 1.3 miles. Turn left onto McKinney Road, which becomes Minden Ave., and follow it 0.5 mile. Take a right across a small bridge to the Minden trailhead.

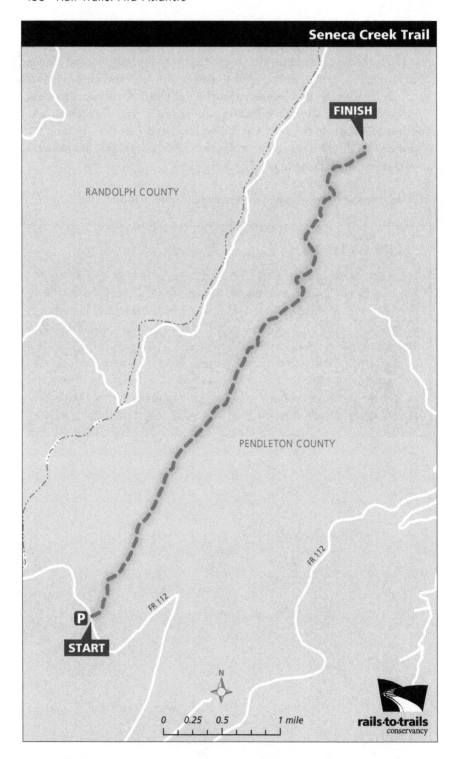

Located in the Spruce Knob–Seneca Rocks National Recreation Area of the Monongahela National Forest—a hot spot for mountain biking and rock climbing—the Seneca Creek Trail is a scenic feast of streams, meadows, forests, and waterfalls. Unlike other rail-trails in the national forest, this out-and-back route shows characteristics typical of former railroad corridors: It is flat and provides a relatively steady, easy hike that is doable with a mountain bike.

The trail is part of the 70-mile Spruce Knob–Seneca Creek Backcountry trail system. At 4,863 feet, Spruce Knob is West Virginia's highest peak. While all the interconnecting trails are well marked with blue diamond blazes, do not expect the additional 65 miles of hiking to be so gentle.

The route follows Seneca Creek, a fast-flowing, spring-fed mountain stream, whose clean, crystal water can be heard and seen nearly everywhere along the trail. From

County
Pendleton

Endpoints
FR 112 to Upper Seneca Creek Falls (Monongahela National Forest, near Riverton)

Mileage
5

Type
Rail-Trail

Roughness Index
3

Surface
Dirt

The obligatory stream crossing on Seneca Creek Trail is worth it for the trail's dramatic finale: Upper Seneca Creek Falls.

the trailhead, you'll immediately pass through meadows and spruce groves. A few miles in, you will encounter hardwoods. A canopy of maple, beech, birch, and cherry creates a natural tunnel, offering a wide array of color in the fall and shade in the summer.

Multiple creek crossings dot the path, and there are no footbridges, so come prepared to get your feet wet. Near the trail's end, the last, and most rewarding, creek crossing brings you to the 30-foot Upper Seneca Creek Falls. The spectacular falls are the highest on Seneca Creek and offer a dramatic finale to this hike.

CONTACT: www.fs.usda.gov/mnf

DIRECTIONS

From Elkins, take US 33/WV 55 E 44.5 miles to Briery Gap Road/CR 33/4, and turn right. Follow Briery Gap Road approximately 2.5 miles until you reach FR 112, and turn right. This steep, narrow gravel road is not maintained in winter. Drive approximately 11.5 miles until you reach the trailhead on your right. Limited parking is available.

The South Prong Trail is a remote, rugged rail-trail that offers a moderate, though sometimes quite hilly, hike. There are two very distinct sections of this trail: One section is boggy, while the other is steep and forested.

Traversing the Flatrock Plains and Roaring Plains of Monongahela National Forest, this trail follows old logging corridors for part of its route. The western end follows approximately 3 miles of terraced railbeds along a flat corridor for a short while before heading uphill, or downhill, to the next terrace of railbeds, located almost vertically 15–25 feet below or above you.

The South Prong Trail is blazed with blue diamonds, but be careful if you start from the eastern end. The blazes marking the turnoff points through the terraced railbeds can be easy to overlook. The trail reaches an elevation of 4,130 feet and then levels off, following the Eastern

Counties
Pendleton, Randolph

Endpoints
FR 19 West to FR 19 East
(Monongahela National
Forest, near Davis)

Mileage
4.5

Type
Rail-Trail

Roughness Index
3

Surface
Dirt

Springtime brings blooming rhododendrons, West Virginia's state flower, to the South Prong Trail.

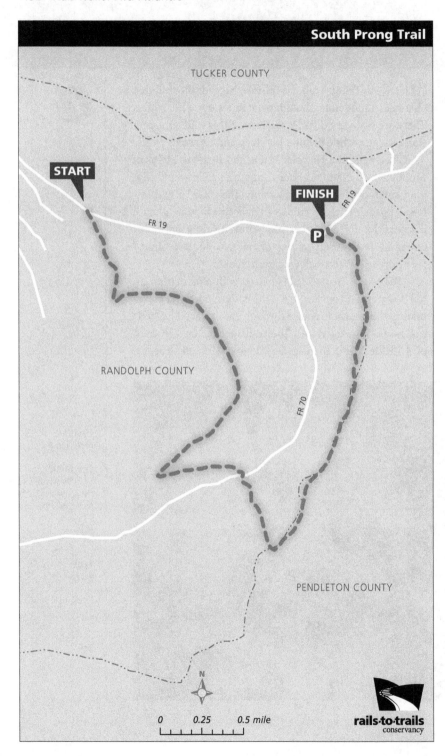

Continental Divide. Near the midsection, you will cross Forest Road 70, a quiet road, and enter into different terrain: a landscape that is rocky and wet, with beautiful flora. Red spruces are reclaiming the once deforested area, while azaleas, blueberries, rhododendrons (West Virginia's state flower), and thickets of mountain laurels surround you.

To turn your out-and-back trip into a loop, consider parking your car at the western trailhead and following the trail east. Once you've completed the hike, walk west along quiet FR 19 for 1.7 miles. This will take you from the eastern trailhead back to the western trailhead, where you can close the loop.

CONTACT: www.fs.usda.gov/mnf

DIRECTIONS

From Elkins, take US 33/WV 55 E for 22.4 miles to WV 32 and turn left, now heading north. After 3.9 miles, turn right onto Bonner Mountain Road/CR 32, and follow it 4.9 miles. After crossing over Red Creek, make a sharp left and then an immediate right to turn onto Laneville Road/CR 45/4. After 1.1 miles, this road turns into FR 19, a steep, narrow gravel road. Be careful navigating it. Go approximately 1.3 miles, and you will see the South Prong/Boar's Nest Trailheads. Turn right into a small parking area near the west end of the trail. To reach the east end, continue on FR 19 another 1.7 miles until you reach a small trailhead with parking on the right.

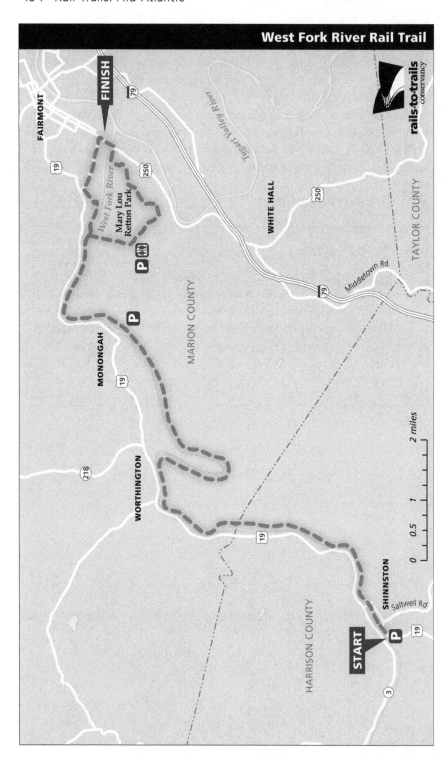

West Virginia's West Fork River Rail Trail provides a snapshot of some of the most beautiful scenery in this region. The trail's path was once used by the far-reaching Baltimore & Ohio Railroad to deliver coal. Today's plans, however, are to transport people and link this rail-trail to the American Discovery Trail.

Shortly after its start in picturesque Shinnston, the route reaches the rippling West Fork River and its cliffs and forests. Close to the Harrison and Marion County border, you will pass a historical railroad bridge that spans the river. The trail travels through some wooded passages, and then it opens up to a park, where children play baseball and softball and fisherman vie for the prized catch below the dam.

A few miles beyond the park, you cross a railroad bridge and return to the wooded haven of the trail. At the town of Norway, you have the option of going another 0.5

Counties
Harrison, Marion

Endpoints
Mahlon St./S. Pike St. near US 19 (Shinnston) to Edgeway Dr. near US 19 (Fairmont)

Mileage
18.3

Type
Rail-Trail

Roughness Index
2

Surface
Cinder, Crushed Stone, Gravel

The small town of Monongah, directly across the river from the trail, has a storied history.

mile to a stunning wooden bridge, or you can head to the on-road section of trail before you reach the bridge and access Mary Lou Retton Park, which offers recreational fields, parking, restrooms, and the West Virginia Miners Memorial. Pay close attention for the turnoff for the park: Heading toward Fairmont, the turnoff (CR 56/3) is on the right. After turning off the trail, turn left before the intersection with Old Monongah Road.

If you prefer to skip the park, you can continue on road, taking lefts on Old Monongah Road, Mary Lou Retton Drive, Fairmont Avenue (US 250), Country Club Road, and finally Edgeway Drive. This loop will lead you back to the off-road portion of trail and to the wooden bridge to cross back to your original turn-off. This loop is only recommended for individuals comfortable with on-road riding in light to medium traffic.

CONTACT: shinnstonwv.com/index.cfm/parks-events/west-fork-river-rail-trail

DIRECTIONS

The starting point in Shinnston is accessible from US 19 on the southern end of town. To reach Shinnston, take I-79 to Exit 125 (Shinnston/Saltwell Road), turn left (west) onto WV 131/ Benedum Dr., and proceed 0.5 mile to the gas station. Turn left onto Saltwell Road/WV 131, and follow this 6.4 miles to US 19 in Shinnston. Turn right onto US 19/Pike St. and drive six blocks. Turn left onto Mahlon St. at St. Ann's Catholic Church, before the bridge across the West Fork River. Go one block and park on the street. The trail begins under the US 19 bridge.

To reach the northern end in Fairmont, your best bet is to actually park in Monongah. From I-79, take Exit 132, and turn left (north) onto US 250/White Hall Blvd. Follow US 250 for 1.2 miles, and turn left onto Holbert Road/Monkey Wrench Hollow. After 1.2 miles, turn left onto Booths Creek Road. In another 0.6 mile, turn right to remain on Booths Creek. Take a slight left onto Bridge St. in 0.4 mile. Just before the West Fork River, turn off Bridge St. into the parking lot. The trail is just off the lot.

56 West Fork Trail

The West Fork Trail is a pleasant, 22-mile path that snakes its way through a remote mountain setting and follows the West Fork River for most of its route. The soothing rumble of the river complements the trail's serene environment. This is a great path for biking, but the surface is primarily ballast left over from the rail corridor, so leave your road bike at home. The route begins in the small community of Glady. Even though the trail appears to be flat, you will find yourself on a gentle decline as the trail follows the river downstream from Glady. For the first 5 miles, the path takes a higher route above the western side of the river and pops in and out of small groves of conifers, offering great views of the surrounding hills. It also intersects with other hiking trails within the forest, including the High Falls Trail, if you want to get your waterfall fix. The West Fork Trail then levels out with the

This trail, popular with fishermen, meanders through lush valleys.

County
Randolph

Endpoints
Highland St. at WV 92
(Durbin) to Glady

Mileage
22

Type
Rail-Trail

Roughness Index
2

Surface
Ballast, Crushed Stone,
Gravel

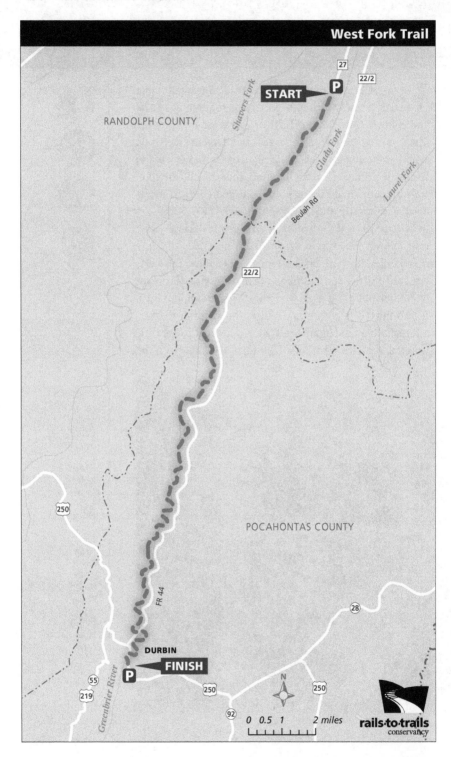

West Fork Trail

27

22/2

START P

RANDOLPH COUNTY

Shavers Fork

Glady Fork

Laurel Fork

Beulah Rd

22/2

POCAHONTAS COUNTY

250

28

FR 44

DURBIN

P **FINISH**

Greenbrier River

55

219

250

92

250

N

0   0.5   1   2 miles

rails·to·trails
conservancy

river and travels the remaining 17 miles to the town of Durbin, following the river southward.

Meandering through the mountains, the trail and the river make sweeping 180-degree turns through a tight valley surrounded by steep hillsides. The West Fork River is a popular fishing spot, and you are bound to see a number of anglers along the way. The trail comes to an end in the town of Durbin, a quiet Appalachian town that has wonderful little lunch spots and a nice Main Street corridor. A bonus 1.3-mile rail-trail, the Widney Park Rail-Trail, can be accessed right in downtown Durbin.

CONTACT: **www.fs.usda.gov/mnf**

DIRECTIONS

To reach the northern trailhead from Elkins, take US 33/WV 55 E for 12 miles, and make a right onto CR 27/Glady Road. Follow it for approximately 9.5 miles to the town of Glady. When you come to the intersection of Glady Road and CR 22, continue straight on Glady through the stop sign, and follow the road for approximately 0.75 mile to where it dead-ends. The trailhead will be directly in front of you.

To reach the southern trailhead from Elkins, take US 219/US 250 about 18 miles south to Huttonsville. Merge onto US 250 going south, and follow it 18.7 miles to Durbin. Look for the trailhead on the right at the intersection with Highland St. about 1 mile before you reach the town. Just before the trailhead entrance, you'll find a small driveway, where limited parking is available on the side.

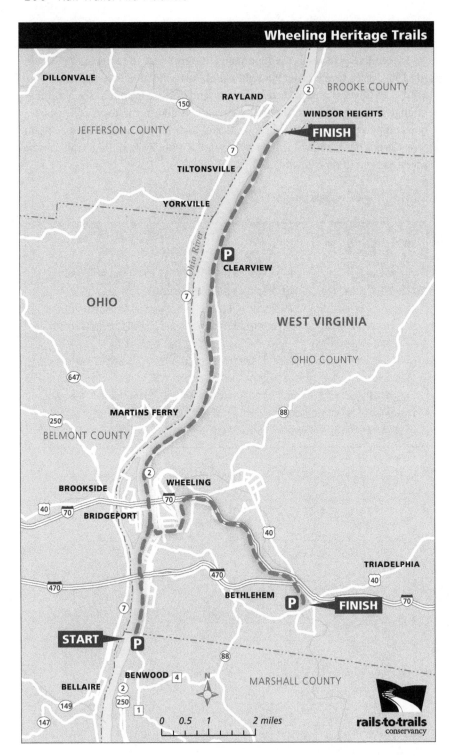

Wheeling Heritage Trails

DILLONVALE

BROOKE COUNTY

RAYLAND

150

JEFFERSON COUNTY

WINDSOR HEIGHTS

7

FINISH

TILTONSVILLE

YORKVILLE

Ohio River

P

CLEARVIEW

7

OHIO

WEST VIRGINIA

OHIO COUNTY

647

88

MARTINS FERRY

250

BELMONT COUNTY

BROOKSIDE

WHEELING

40 70

70

BRIDGEPORT

TRIADELPHIA

40

40

470

470

40

70

BETHLEHEM

P **FINISH**

7

START P

88

BENWOOD 4

2

BELLAIRE

250 N

149

1 MARSHALL COUNTY

147

0 0.5 1 2 miles

rails·to·trails
conservancy

The Wheeling Heritage Trails running on the former Baltimore & Ohio line are known locally as two trails that connect in downtown Wheeling: the Ohio River Trail and the Wheeling Creek Trail. The route is flat and paved, and beautiful signs along the way provide a self-guided tour of Wheeling's past.

The Ohio River Trail segment runs 11 miles from 48th Street at Water Street in South Wheeling north to Pike Island Locks and Dam in Clearview. The route provides an urban escape and an opportunity to soak up local history and modern industry in this historical city. The path follows the eastern bank of the Ohio River, once the lifeblood of the city's manufacturing industry. Barges still go up and down the river, and with good timing and patience, you can watch one progress through the series of locks. Take a break to rest on a bench, and you will be

A market along the waterfront section of the trail

County
Ohio

Endpoints
Short Creek Road at WV 2 (Short Creek) to 48th and Water Sts. (South Wheeling) to Lava Ave. at Jr. Ave. (Elm Grove)

Mileage
16.5

Type
Rail-Trail

Roughness Index
1

Surface
Asphalt

rewarded with a splendid view of the river and wildlife. This trail connects to the Wheeling Creek Trail at Heritage Port.

From downtown Wheeling, the Wheeling Creek Trail heads east to Elm Grove for 5 miles. Along the way, you'll cross high above Wheeling Creek on the Hempfield Viaduct and pass through Hempfield Tunnel, built in 1904. This segment of the Wheeling Heritage Trails is less urban and meanders along a wooded corridor.

It is worth noting that at the trail's northern terminus, you can pick up the nearly 7-mile Brooke Pioneer Trail (see page 144) and continue your journey all the way to Wellsburg for a more substantial ride.

CONTACT: wheelingwv.gov/parksandrecreation.php

DIRECTIONS

To get to the starting point in downtown Wheeling, take I-70 to Exit 1A. Travel north on Main St., which becomes River Road and then Warwood Ave., for 5.7 miles, and look for Pike Island Locks and Dam on the left. The parking lot is in front of the dam.

The endpoint is located at the intersection of 48th St. and Water St. in downtown Wheeling. Take I-70 to Exit 1B. Follow US 250 S for 3.1 miles. Take the exit toward Boggs Run Road/WV 1. Follow Marshall St. N for 0.2 mile, and turn left onto Second St. Take a right onto Water St., and the trailhead will be 0.3 mile ahead at the intersection with 48th St.

To access the eastern trail terminus in Elm Grove, take I-70 E from downtown Wheeling for 3.5 miles. Take Exit 4/WV 88 S toward Elm Grove. Merge onto National Road/US 40, and continue for 0.4 mile. Take a right onto Jr. Ave. and a sharp right onto Lava Ave. After 0.2 mile, the street name changes to Community St.; follow it another 0.3 mile to access the parking lot.

Index

Photo Credits

Page i: Virginia Department of Conservation and Recreation; *page iii:* Ray C. Thompson; *page 7:* James McGinnis; *page 9:* James McGinnis; *page 11:* Deb Morris; *page 15:* James McGinnis; *page 19:* Michel Gagnon; *page 21:* Rails-to-Trails Conservancy/Barbara Richey; *page 23:* Jim Hopkins; *page 27:* Rails-to-Trails Conservancy; *page 28:* Rails-to-Trails Conservancy; *page 29:* David C. Stone; *page 35:* Ray C. Thompson; *page 37:* Jim Hopkins; *page 41:* Lynn Bashaw; *page 43:* Michel Park; *page 47:* Rails-to-Trails Conservancy; *page 49:* Rails-to-Trails Conservancy; *page 53:* Rails-to-Trails Conservancy; *page 55:* John Reeg; *page 59:* Rails-to-Trails Conservancy/Barbara Richey; *page 61:* Steve Earley; *page 65:* Mike Mulhearn; *page 67:* Paul Ericson; *page 71:* Regina Worrell; *page 73:* Chip Early; *page 77:* Billy Hall; *page 79:* Erik Kaldor; *page 83:* Virginia State Parks; *page 85:* Steve Tatum; *page 89:* Alleghany County Parks and Recreation; *page 91:* Virginia Department of Transportation; *page 95:* Diana Norgaard; *page 97:* Thomas Cizauskas; *page 99:* Daniel Mott; *page 100:* Daniel Mott; *page 101:* William Couch; *page 104:* Elvert Barnes; *page 105:* Tom Bilcze; *page 109:* Sam Doyle; *page 111:* Joseph Malak; *page 115:* Emily Harper; *page 117:* Maureen Hannan; *page 120:* Maureen Hannan; *page 121:* Milo Bateman; *page 125:* Virginia Department of Conservation and Recreation; *page 127:* Virginia Department of Conservation and Recreation; *page 129:* Alice Crain; *page 131:* Rails-to-Trails Conservancy/Barbara Richey; *page 133:* Hugh Morris; *page 137:* Jeff Wimer; *page 139:* Kit Thomas; *page 140:* Kit Thomas; *page 141:* Mark Mervine; *page 145:* Duncan Brown; *page 147:* Jim Mullhaupt; *page 151:* Aaron Welch; *page 153:* Kim Hudnall Richmond; *page 157:* Jake Lynch; *page 159:* Rails-to-Trails Conservancy; *page 161:* Rails-to-Trails Conservancy; *page 163:* David Fulmer; *page 167:* Teresa Cheek; *page 169:* Jim Hopkins; *page 171:* Jeff Turner; *page 173:* Jeff Wimer; *page 175:* Mike Jennings; *page 179:* Rails-to-Trails Conservancy/ Katie Harris; *page 181:* Spencer Riddile; *page 185:* Agatha Thiel; *page 189:* Ron Shearer; *page 191:* Gertrude Kalmar; *page 195:* Phil Sparks; *page 197:* Darrell Young; *page 201:* Heather Ausher.

Support Rails-to-Trails Conservancy

The nation's leader in helping communities transform unused rail lines and connecting corridors into multiuse trails, Rails-to-Trails Conservancy (RTC) depends on the support of its members and donors to create access to healthy outdoor experiences.

Your donation will help support programs and services that have helped put more than 22,000 rail-trail miles on the ground. Every day, RTC provides vital assistance to communities to develop and maintain trails throughout the country. In addition, RTC advocates for trail-friendly policies, promotes the benefits of rail-trails, and defends rail-trail laws in the courts.

Join online at **railstotrails.org,** or mail your donation to Rails-to-Trails Conservancy, 2121 Ward Court NW, Fifth Floor, Washington, D.C. 20037.

Rails-to-Trails Conservancy is a 501(c)(3) nonprofit organization, and contributions are tax deductible.

Find your next trail adventure on TrailLink

Visit TrailLink.com today.

TrailLink
by Rails-to-Trails Conservancy